Unity Conscious Leadership
interdependent growth and transformation

From a Buddhist Perspective

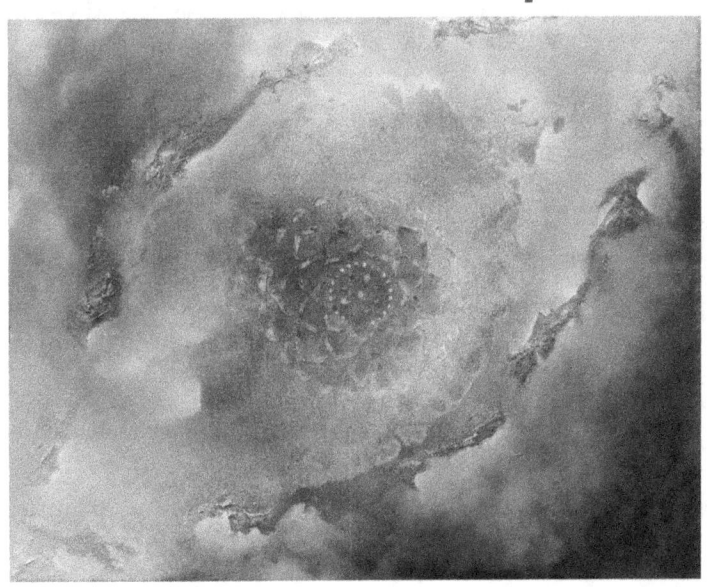

SEEDS FOR HEALTH, HAPPINESS & PEACE
(How to overcome and transform crises and hardships to gain personal, cultural and professional leadership)

Joyce Z. Wazirali

Unity Conscious Leadership™(Interdependent Growth and Transformation): From a Buddhist Perspective

© 2021 Joyce Z. Wazirali

Published by Make Your Mark Global Partners, LTD

The purpose of this book is not to give medical advice, nor to give a prescription for the use of any technique as a form of treatment for any physical, medical, psychological, or emotional condition. The information in this book does not replace the advice of a physician, either directly or indirectly. It is intended only as general information and education. In the event that you use any of the information in this book for yourself, as is your constitutional right, the authors and publisher assume no responsibility for your actions. No expressed or implied guarantee of the effect of the use of any of the recommendations can be given. The author and publisher are not liable or responsible for any loss or damage allegedly arising from any information in this book. Many of the names and personal details have been changed to protect the privacy of individuals.

Without limiting the rights under copyright reserved above, no part of this publication may be reproduced, stored in, or introduced into a retrieval system, or transmitted in any form or by any means (electronic, mechanical, photocopying, recording, or otherwise), without the prior written permission of the copyright owner.

The scanning, uploading, and distribution of this book via the Internet or any other means without the permission of the publisher are illegal and punishable by law. Please purchase only authorized electronic editions and do not participate in or encourage any electronic piracy of copyrightable materials. Your support of the author's rights is appreciated. And karma will get you if you violate this anyway!

While the author and publisher have made every effort to provide accurate information regarding references and Internet addresses at the time of publication, the author and publisher do not assume responsibility for errors or changes that occur after publication. The author and publisher also do not assume any responsibility for third-party websites and/or their content.

Publisher: Make Your Mark Global, LTD

Las Vegas, Nevada

Pages - 187

Trade Paperback ISBN 978-1-7356790-9-9

Hardcover ISBN 978-1-7356790-4-4

Ebook ISBN 978-1-7356790-5-1

Subjects: Business, Family

Summary: In *Unity Conscious Leadership*™, author Joyce Z. Wazirali takes you on a journey of awareness and discovery of the causes and effects of conflicts and crises. As a practitioner of many years standing, she reveals the secrets of the complex dynamic of relationships and cultural issues. By using various disciplines and illustrating the theories with practical examples from her work, Joyce shows how individuals and companies can use crises and obstructive situations to break through perpetuating patterns in order to grow and thrive again. Thanks to her unique approach, she is often able to detect problems others have missed.

MAKE YOUR MARK GLOBAL PUBLISHING, LTD

USA

'For my children Eric and Amy, my wise mirrors, whom I love very much.'

*'The lives of all people are one with the universe.
All movements of the universe contribute to
the individuality of each person.*

*In other words, each person is a microcosm,
a unique reflection of the macro cosmos;
in fact, the individual includes everything.*

That is why every person is precious and irreplaceable.'

- Daisaku Ikeda

(The Wisdom of the Lotus Sutra - a discussion part 2, 88)

*We are not in an era of change,
we are the creators,
standing at the threshold of
a new era of health, happiness and peace.*

- Joyce Z. Wazirali -

Table of Contents

Foreword ix
Introduction 1
Making the Invisible, Visible (A Mystical Voyage) 9

A NEW ERA, A NEW PARADIGM OF LEADERSHIP 14
Chapter 1: Paradigms, Patterns and Paradoxes 15
- *Two Paradigms* 15
- *Patterns and Paradoxes* 23
- *Breaking Through Patterns and Paradoxes* 31

Chapter 2: Interdependent Growth and Transformation 37
- *Triggers are the Keys to Transformation* 37
- *Unity of Person and Environment* 40
- *The Law of Cause and Effect* 42
- *The All-Pervasive Influence of the Past, Present and Future* 44
- *The Power of Forgiveness: Turning Poison into Medicine* 47
- *Projection is Perception* 50
- *The Coherence and Alchemy of Life* 53

Chapter 3: The Intelligence of the Heart 61
- *Ancient Wisdom and Modern Science About the Heart* 61
- *The Lotus Sutra or Heart Sutra* 63
- *Scientific Evidence About the Heart* 64

PERSONAL LEADERSHIP 68
Chapter 4: The Nine Layers of Consciousness of the Lotus Sutra 69
- *The principle of the Nine Layers of Consciousness* 69
- *Explanation of the Nine Layers of Consciousness* 73
- *Relative and Absolute Happiness* 79

- General 81

Chapter 5: Unity Conscious Leadership™ Concept of Suffering and Transformation 83
- Concept of Personal Suffering and Transformation 83
- Explanation of the Layers of Suffering and Transformation............ 84
- Layers of Suffering 85
- Layer of Transformation 97
- General 97
- Merging Eastern Wisdom with Western Knowledge 98
- Seven Steps for Personal Unity Conscious Leadership™ 100

CULTURAL LEADERSHIP 101
Chapter 6: Leadership from a Buddhist Perspective 103
- *My Early Experiences With Cultures* 103
- *The Emergence of Culture* 107
- *Influence of Those Who are Responsible*... 109
- *Who Makes the Culture?*... 110

Chapter 7: Unity Conscious Leadership™ Concept of Cultural Transformation.. 115
- My Experience on the Cultural Level with CEOs as Culture Influencers... 115
- Unity Conscious Leadership™ concept of Cultural Transformation... 118
- Explanation of the Concept of Cultural Transformation 118
- Miscommunication 124
- Interpersonal Behaviour and Patterns... 128
- Intertwining of Personal and Organizational Undercurrent 129
- Layer Six, the Transformational Level 135
- Why Most Cultural Change Projects Fail 138
- The Complex of Personal and Organizational Dynamics 141
- Tips for Personal and Cultural Development................................... 142

- The Keys to the Solutions.. 148
- Eight Steps for Cultural Change With Unity Conscious Leadership™... 149

PROFESSIONAL LEADERSHIP.. **151**
Chapter 8: The Truth Behind the Facts **153**
- *Discovering the Truth Behind the Facts* *153*
- *My Legacy from the Plasa Group*...................................... *157*
- *Traits and Mastery*.. *159*

Chapter 9: Last but not Least... **165**
- *Revealing Our Diamond*... *165*
- *Transformation*.. *166*
- *Future Leadership*.. *168*

Reference List / Reading List... **169**
About the Author **173**

Foreword

At the time of the publication of this book, we are currently living through multiple unprecedented crises — personal, professional, cultural and even planetary crises. With so much chaos and uncertainty it is clear that we need some form of advanced, conscious leadership. Between global warming, political shake ups and social meltdowns our world has been turned inside out. Never before has the entire world gone through such dramatic social, cultural, personal and political upheavals all at the same time. Sadly, much of the turmoil was man made. This has opened our eyes to how interdependent we really are. What happens on the other side of the planet has a direct impact on us.

Our personal and collective vulnerability has been exposed as we have seen police officers senselessly murder of innocent people on TV and social media, often without justice. Mass school shootings, racially motivated hate crimes, and blatant gender discrimination have made many of us afraid to be go outside. The #metoo movement brought more attention to the widespread abuse of power by men, inspiring women everywhere to call for the end of the patriarchy. A rallying cry across the globe can be heard for more equitable treatment of all people in all areas of life. We have arrived at the end of an era of forced silence.

Because these dark times threaten our safety and even our identity, we naturally look to leaders for help. Unfortunately many of the people in positions of leadership, whether in corporations, schools or families, do not possess the skills or experience to guide us out of the darkness. Our collective need for conscious leadership is more apparent than ever. This means we need to develop a new skill set and perspective within ourselves, our organizations and governments.

Until new leaders step up, each of us is being called to take new responsibility for our lives. It is clear that, at present, we cannot solely rely on governments, manufacturers, or pharmaceuticals for our wellbeing. We must acknowledge our personal imprint on the planet and be more conscious of how we interact with others. The time has come for us to take accountability for our part in the world drama. In other words, whether we consider ourselves spiritual or not, we are all awakening to our interconnectedness. And this is a beautiful thing to behold.

According to author, coach and consultant, Joyce Z. Wazirali, a new paradigm of leadership is emerging, one in which we recognize that we are not separate, one that acknowledges the incredible potential we each possess to become leaders. Joyce describes Unity Conscious Leadership™ as an approach to looking at the world through the lens of interdependence as we put aside the outdated mindset of duality.

When I met Joyce two years ago for another book project I was impressed and inspired by her passion for helping make this world a better place by changing our perspective on life. As she shared some of her own awakening journey with me it was clear that she possesses a deep understanding of the spiritual side of leadership development, as she has not only lived it herself, but also taught thousands of people along the way.

As you'll read in this book, the Unity Conscious Leadership ™ perspective includes three key elements. Unity, or oneness, is the fundamental understanding that we are all interconnected, interdependent and influencing each other continuously. As we all are conscious beings we can increase our consciousness by perceiving our outer world as a reflection of our inner world. And recognizing that everyone is a leader we see that we each have the ability to find answers and solutions within ourselves.

Joyce has used her professional experience from high level corporate consulting to individual and group facilitation and distilled into this book a framework that will help you uncover more of your hidden potential. And this is the perfect moment to do it. This moment is a turning point in our collective and personal history. It offers us the opportunity to look deep within to challenge our assumptions and beliefs and become more aligned with our core values and soul. Rather than repeating the errors of the past we are guided to take advantage of this moment as a catalyst for growth.

Combining the spiritual wisdom of the East with practical business insights from the West, Joyce emphasizes that a Buddhist perspective will open up more possibilities for deep healing and transformation. By sharing some wisdom of one of the Buddha's famous teachings, the Lotus Sutra, Joyce shows us how we can break free from our past programming that leads to frustration and clashes in culture. She has been expertly guiding clients to explore their traumas to release the pain of the past, liberating them to evolve and lead from the heart. And now she is here to guide you.

I believe the Lotus Sutra is the perfect backdrop for learning about our inherent potential for conscious evolution and heart-centered leadership. It is said that the Buddha taught that even the most corrupt person can hope for and attain enlightenment. And every obstacle or difficulty offers the opportunity for growth if we are willing to examine our part in it. As the saying goes, with wisdom and applying skillful means we can change poison into medicine.

The path Joyce lays out for you in this book will set you on a journey of self-discovery, healing and empowerment. Whether you are leading a nation, a company, or a family, Unity Conscious Leadership™ will support you in becoming the best version of yourself as you lead with heart and soul. May this book serve you and inspire you.

Many blessings,
Andrea Pennington, MD

Introduction

Unity Conscious Leadership™
makes the invisible, visible
the unknown, known
the impossible, possible
creates healthy people, happy societies and a peaceful world.

– Joyce Z. Wazirali –

Time of crisis, time for change

At this moment, as I prepare to publish this book, the whole world is in a deep crisis. We are busy fighting against the new SARS-CoV-2, the coronavirus which is commonly known as Covid-19. The crisis manifests itself on multiple levels, such as health, economics, politics, social, emotional, and more.

This is not the first time we find ourselves fighting an (invisible) enemy. Although invisible to our eyes, it is our focus. The battle to protect ourselves is pulling down all the structures we have built for our safety, health, happiness and peace faster than we created them.

First of all, I am very sorry for all the people who are suffering illness, or loss of their loved ones, with no opportunity to comfort each other or to say goodbye. They are enveloped in a sense of powerlessness. Businesses are obliged to shut down. People are living in poverty and uncertainty, not knowing what to do.

This is a collective situation that affects the whole world in many ways. Therefore, we need to find a collective solution. The virus brings us back to self-reflection and forces us to change direction. The imbalance of the dynamic is not only outside us but is also *inside* us. The outer world is like a mirror of our inner world. Thus, we find the time to come closer to our own nature.

In this book you will find valuable theories, tools, stories and information to enable you to discover how to reflect on a collective way forward.

Times of crisis, times of possibilities

In Greek and Chinese, the word "crisis" has two meanings: 'problems' and 'possibilities'.

Problems persist if you look for solutions outside of yourself. But by finding solutions within yourself, you create possibilities for a new reality. You cannot change the behaviour of other people. You can only change the way you handle situations and view your world. That requires a mind shift. A paradigm shift from *Dualism* to Unity Conscious Leadership™.

Paradigm shift from *Dualism* to Unity Conscious Leadership™

Dualism, the old paradigm

Here lies the root cause of obstructive patterns and paradoxes, the source of conflicts and crises. People and organizations often struggle with repetitive patterns of obstacles and counter currents, believing that they are separate and independent of their environment. They look for causes and solutions outside themselves, and try to break through patterns with a temporary fix by means of trial and error. They look at themselves and their world through the lens of *dualism*.

Unity Conscious Leadership™, the new paradigm for Future Leadership

Maybe you are thinking, **how can I** be responsible for the change in my environment when things are happening **to** me? That's what some of my clients asked when they first met me. Many clients now have a different view of themselves, their lives and their environment through my guidance. They use the obstacles in their lives for their own growth and transformation.

According to Unity Conscious Leadership™, everyone is a leader, regardless of rank and social position.

Unity Conscious Leadership™ is the new paradigm or model of leadership, to overcome and transform crises for personal, cultural and professional growth for more health, happiness and peace.

The way to achieve Unity Conscious Leadership™ is through **interdependent growth and transformation**. In Buddhism, *'turn poison into medicine'* means using obstacles as a springboard for growth and transformation.

My mission with this book

I believe
that the religion of the future
will be
a cosmic religion.

– Albert Einstein –

With this book I hope to inspire you and give you insights about the complexity of life and how to take a step forward by breaking through obstructive patterns and paradoxes.

My aim is to nurture the seeds of health, happiness and peace you already have in you. By sharing my experiences and insights with you I hope those seeds will grow.

What helped me to give words to Unity Conscious Leadership™ was the practice and deepening understanding of Nichiren Buddhism.[1]

In this book, I will reveal a 'glimpse' of the complex intertwining of:

1. *The coherence of life* (based on the Eastern wisdom of the Lotus Sutra[2], created 2,600 years ago by Shakyamuni Buddha (also known as Gautama Siddhartha),

2. *The alchemy of life* (the Western knowledge of system dynamics, quantum physics and collective field), and

---

[1] The wisdom of the Lotus Sutra was distributed through Buddha (2,600 BC) in India, T'ien-t'ai Chih-i (538–597) in China, Nichiren Daishonin (1222-1282), Tsunesaburo Makiguchi (1871-1944), Jose Toda (1900-1958) and Daisaku Ikeda (1928- present) in Japan. It began to reach the rest of the world in 1960 and is now practiced by over 12 million people in 201 countries and territories.

The mission of Nichiren Buddhism is world peace and happiness for all who live, by observing the Universal laws and working on self-reflection, awareness and personal growth in the midst of society. Answers and the keys to solutions are in ourselves and in our hearts.

[2] After passing on teachings which included how to relieve people of their suffering, many forms of yoga and meditation, Buddha sought answers about the coherence of life. He explained this in the Lotus Sutra. He concluded that the human heart is a treasure tower where both pain and the ability to **achieve absolute happiness** are stored. The human heart is sensitive, versatile and rich. It also includes the capacity to deliver incredible performance.

In the Lotus Sutra, Buddha also explains how the complex mystical law of the universe works and that *we all are the mystical law*.

3. *The layers of suffering and transformation* (which I have obtained through more than three decades of experience in the field of people and business growth, and transformation from the perspective of Unity Conscious Leadership™).

Experience expert

> *The whole world is within you.*
> *If you know how to look and learn.*
> *The door is already there and the key is in your hand.*
> *No one on earth can give you either the key,*
> *or open the door for you.*
> *Except you.*
>
> – Jiddu Krishnamurti –

My name is **Joyce Z. Wazirali**, founder and CEO of Unity Conscious Leadership™. I am a consultant, coach, counsellor, trainer, speaker, author and entrepreneur. I offer tailor-made leadership programmes for individuals and leaders so they can change their environment and conquer personal and cultural issues from the perspective of Unity Conscious Leadership™.

For more than three decades I have been successfully guiding more than 1,000 individuals and CEOs with the 'lens' of Unity Conscious Leadership™. For six years, I was a member of the supervisory board of a corporation with 600 General Practitioners.

At the age of 23, I was co-founder, CEO and HR-manager of the Plasa Group, a company in business services. Within 13 years we built a successful company with 80 staff members. Our clients and staff members were our greatest ambassadors.

The 'lens' of Unity Conscious Leadership™ was one of the success factors of the Plasa Group.

I had always used this 'lens' unconsciously until I discovered it while writing this book.

Since my childhood I have seen patterns and interdependence everywhere in nature and between people. The patterns made future events predictable to me. Seeing through patterns makes it easy and quick for me to "put my finger on the sore spot" by asking a few questions and deploying the right guidance to break through and transform obstructive patterns. I thought everyone could see that. In retrospect, it turned out to be my gift.

For whom?

Life is a school for learning.
And experience is the best teacher.

– Joyce Z. Wazirali –

This book is for anyone who wants to *transcend mutual differences to create unity*.

If you are struggling with:

- Relationships or situations in life or business
- Repeatedly falling into old habits or patterns
- Problems despite therapy, coaching, working on limiting beliefs or using psychedelic resources
- Direction or leadership in life or business

Or you want more growth of:
- Potential, resilience and adaptability
- Health, happiness and peace in life

Sources

Over the years I have followed many training courses, gained experience and in combination with my dreams, visions and insights I will share the knowledge with you in my own words. Where I have quoted from a book, I will state the source. At the end of this book, you will find a reading list of resources which have inspired me.

For three decades I have had many clients. I mostly remember the stories but not always their names. For the clients I still remember, I have changed the names in the practical examples I mention.

Where I have mentioned 'intervention' or 'session' in this book, I refer to tailor-made process guidance on mental, social, physical, spiritual and soul levels with the 'lens' of Unity Conscious Leadership™ (UCL™), with the purpose to guide my clients to resolve their problems, develop (self)awareness and unlock potential which enables them to take steps forwards.

Anyone who is willing to learn how to use the 'lens' of UCL™ in daily life or professional environments can follow the year programmes I offer on my websites www.unityconsciousleadership.com and www.eenheidbewustleiderschap.nl.

My motto is:

"Man is a unique and versatile being with answers for a healthy, happy and peaceful life deep inside."

Last but not least

I would like to thank everyone who supported me in the realization of this book. Especially Berthy Stevelmans-Schouten, a wise woman who understands my world and has loaned her listening ear and clarifying questions closer to the core of this book; Dr. Andrea Pennington, a versatile person and my precious soul sister who appeared in my life just at the right moment; and Zoe King, my editor for her wise advice and perseverance.

Joyce Z. Wazirali

MAKING THE INVISIBLE, VISIBLE

A MYSTICAL VOYAGE

*Here is my secret,
a very simple secret.
It is only with your heart that you can see rightly.
What is essential is invisible to the eyes.*

– Antoine De Saint-Exupéry, The Little Prince –

The Day My Voyage Started

*'Today is the only day you can
reconnect with the Universe from a new and higher consciousness.
Do you believe in the intelligence of the universe?
Do you want that?'*

– A 'stranger' in Spain –

It was on February 1st, 2013. I was on holiday in Spain with a good friend of mine.

I gave her a tour of the stupa, a Buddhist temple which I had visited before. After the tour we planned to travel to a picturesque village in the mountains. That day it was very busy with people walking in and outside the stupa. We were walking alongside the stupa in the crowd when I saw a young man with a serene appearance walking towards us. From a distance we already had eye contact. He had a folder in his hands, walked straight to me and started to speak to me in Spanish. He said:

'Hoy es el único día que puedes reconectarse desde una conciencia nueva y superior con el Universo. ¿Crees en la inteligencia del universo? Quieres eso?'

The invisible intelligence in the orchard of my grandmother and my family

The question from this total stranger reminded me of my childhood in Surinam, South America at my grandmother's house. When I was a child, I already knew that we are all connected with each other through a Universal intelligence.

I regularly think back to the times I visited my grandmother as a little girl. She had an orchard with all kinds of tropical trees and fruits. It was a world in which I walked around in wonder and could see the connections and interdependence of all beings in nature. In addition to a variety of trees and shrubs, there were birds, bats, insects and other creatures such as snakes, iguanas and anteaters. Each had its own unique appearance and sound. I was not afraid of them at that time because the animals had never hurt me.

I saw how a hummingbird flew towards a flower, taking nectar with its beak, hovering in one place in the air and then flying backwards. This was the only bird species that could fly forwards, hover in one place in the sky and fly backwards. Other birds picked from the ripe fruit or ate insects that flew into the air or landed on a tree. And then a butterfly came by and fluttered from flower to flower.

Every time I walked around in the orchard, I realized it looked a little different. The fruits on the trees grew and changed colour. Every time I went there, the scents were different. I watched the various types of fruit with amazement and wondered how a banana tree knew what it should look like, how it should make bananas? How could a mango tree know how it should look and how it should make mangos? There must be an invisible intelligence from which nature and beings can tap information.

The interconnectedness and interdependency extended beyond my grandmother's orchard. Without the sun and rain there could be no orchard either. I noticed that if there had been a downpour and the sun was shining, the trees and fruits spread a strong aroma and started to grow faster.

As the seventh in a family with nine children (including two miscarriages), I was able to observe how my parents and brothers and sisters interacted. There were times when situations were predictable for me. As if the dynamics within our family were also influenced by the same invisible intelligence.

Already at a young age I had vivid and predictive dreams, visions and insights that actually manifested. They have become more and more intense over the years. I wonder: 'Is it the same invisible intelligence that provides me with the information or from which I tap?'

For over ten years I spent many hours in my grandmother's orchard until the big move to the Netherlands.

Because of my fascination and connection with nature, the dynamics in my family of origin and the peaceful growing up with different cultures and religions, I have laid the foundation for observing visible and invisible connections.

Mystical experience

I smiled at the young man and said: Yes, I believe in the intelligence of the universe and yes, I would like to reconnect with the universe from a new and higher consciousness.

He said in Spanish to me, 'This is not a joke. I am serious. Are you sure?' I said, 'Yes I'm sure.'

I shook his hand, told him my name and he told his. He took a letter out of his folder and gave it to me with the instruction to read the content of the letter immediately, not on the bus. And let my friend read it after me. I was very curious.

As soon as he handed me the letter he was gone. I followed his instructions and started to read and translated for my friend. Although we were standing still in the middle of a crowd moving around us, it felt like we stood there alone.

We continued our plans to go to the village and to the beach. It was a beautiful sunny day. We enjoyed and had a lot of fun on our journey. In the evening we had dinner in the village close to the stupa. After dinner, we were tired so we headed towards our apartment.

Standing on the top of a road, my friend wanted to take a photo of the galaxy which was clearly visible there. Unfortunately, it was not possible to capture it in the photo.

I wanted to take a photo of the beautiful view of the illuminated villages across the street, where there were still people milling around. We crossed the street and I took my iPhone and determined a good position for a picture. The moment I chose to take the photo, something huge appeared from out of the sky. It was a celestial body! It was fast approaching leaving a trail of light behind.

Making the Invisible, Visible

I shouted, "Wow! what is that?" And I took the photo. My friend standing next to me, looking in the same direction, saw nothing but the illuminated villages. She told me later, she thought it was another one of my jokes. Then I looked at my camera and saw the huge teal-coloured celestial body with a trail of light behind on the photo. My friend looked at the photo and she was staggered at what I had seen and captured on the phone. She said: 'How is this possible? I was looking at the same spot as you, and you saw something so huge. I didn't see it. Even the other people walking around us didn't appear to have seen anything!'

Then I remembered the meeting we'd had with the young man that morning, who said that today was the only day that I could reconnect with the universe from a new and higher consciousness.

My only conclusion was that he came on my path for a reason. And this was the proof that he was sincere.

That night I decided to write a book about leadership from the perspective of unity consciousness. Making the invisible, visible.

This is the photo I took on February the 1st, 2013.

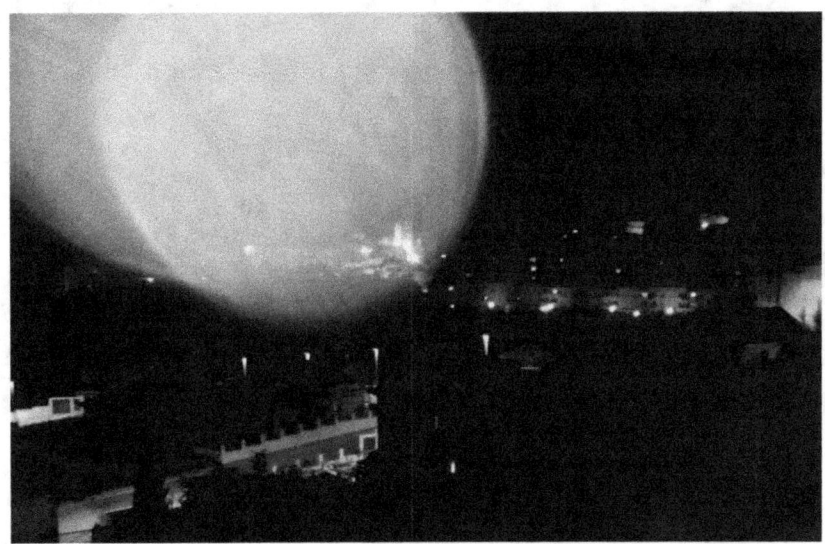

A NEW ERA, A NEW PARADIGM OF LEADERSHIP

CHAPTER 1

PARADIGMS, PATTERNS AND PARADOXES

*Well, you must endure the presence of two or three caterpillars
if you wish
to become acquainted with the butterflies.*

– Antoine de Saint-Exupéry, The Little Prince –

Two Paradigms

***There is nothing out there,
that is not present inside.***

– Goethe –

A paradigm is a generally accepted set of basic assumptions that serve as a starting point.

For example, in the past people thought the earth was flat. They believed that if we reached the end of the earth, we would fall off (old paradigm). Later we discovered that the earth is round, we can never reach the end or fall off (new paradigm).

A paradigm is like a 'lens' someone uses to interpret their world.

The 'lens' of Lena

I had an appointment with Lena. She entered my practice looking very happy. She said: *'Joyce, thank you for the advice you gave me last time. I've tried it and my whole world changed!* There is so much joy and peace within me and also in my environment. I found insights about myself. How I created my old world and affirmed it more and more every day. I thought my environment had to change. But it's me who has to change and make the difference!'

A week earlier, this young woman had come into my practice. She was busy building up her future. She said she missed warm connections with people in her environment. People were not nice to her and she thought they did not like her.

After listening to her story, I asked her what she was thinking about those people. She confessed that she was usually judging and criticizing them.

Then I asked, were you ever connected from heart to heart with them. And she said: *'No! These are not my kind of people.'*

I told her she was looking at the world from the perspective of separateness. But we are not separate. We are interconnected with our environment. Even with mountains, plants and animals. With our thoughts, words and acts we create our own world.

What you see on the outside is a reflection of what's happening inside yourself. If you become aware of what's happening in your inside world, then you know what you can change in yourself to create a new outside world.

She asked me; *'how do I do that? Because I know this situation doesn't make me or my environment happy.'*

I told her, the next time she meets people she is not connected with, she should empty her head, look through her heart and make heart to heart connection with them.

She asked; *'But how can I make a connection? The relationship is so bad after all these years.'* I said, "It's very easy. Just ask, 'how are you doing?'" That was our last conversation.

Today, Lena came back to relate her experience. She was convinced she was the only one who could create her own world. She told me, she did exactly what I told her to do. Lena overcame her anxiety, went to the people she had avoided for so long and asked them how they were doing.

The people she approached started to tell their stories about how they were doing. Within a few minutes they had an easy open conversation and there was connection from both sides. They seemed to be very pleasant people. And Lena enjoyed the evening with them.

She discovered that she was very insecure. The criticism and thoughts about other people were a way to protect her insecurity and to hide her own vulnerability.

Dualism; two philosophies with the same underlying beliefs

a. Individualism

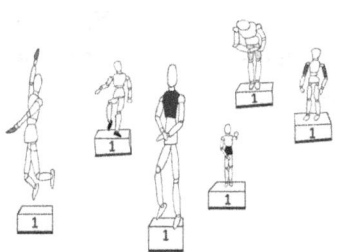

Individualism is a philosophical point of view in which the ideas and rights of the individual are placed above the interests of the community. The essence of individualism is that a group has no rights; only individuals have rights. This is an attitude that is common in Western countries.

The Individualist says, the environment has to adapt to me, and I will operate at the expense of the environment. He or she says, *'my environment must change. Not me.'*

b. Collectivism

Collectivism is a philosophical position where the collective interest exceeds the individual interest. The individual is subordinate to the community or group to which he belongs and conforms to the norms, rules and laws prescribed by the community. This is an attitude that is common in Eastern countries.

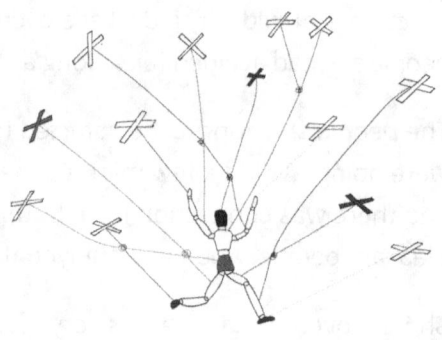

The Collectivist says, people have to adapt to the environment. The environment operates at the expense of the individual. The Individual always adapts and does not show itself. He or she says, *'I have to adapt to the rules of my environment.'*

The underlying beliefs of individualism and collectivism are the same. Both believe that p*eople and their environment are separate from each other* in a dynamic order of hierarchy and inequality. They communicate in a language of opposites such as: good and bad, black and white, us and them, here and there.

Unity Conscious Leadership™

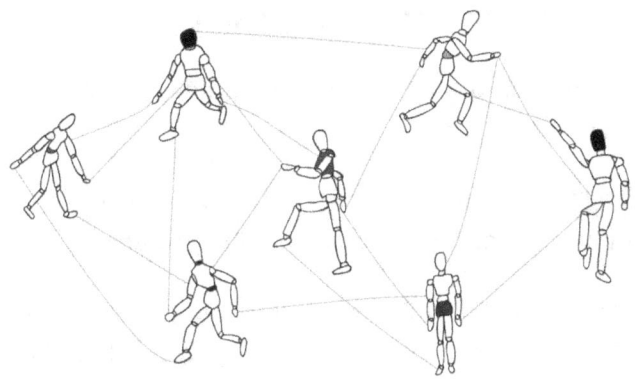

According to Unity Conscious Leadership™ (UCL™), everyone and everything as a whole is **interconnected, interdependent and influencing each other continually.**

What happens in our environment is a reflection of what happens inside ourselves.

To change our environment, we have to make the change in ourselves. By looking for causes and solutions within ourselves, we can break through patterns and transform them with a lasting effect.

The basis of UCL™ is equivalence; everyone and everything is equally important, without ranks and positions. Communicating in a language of oneness such as we, together, with each other.

Life according to....

1. Dualism; creating patterns and paradoxes

(You will find more information about patterns and paradoxes in the next chapter)

Life according to dualism is a journey where you meet people and end up in situations you feel either happy or unhappy about.

From the western perspective, people learn to give each other **feedback** and make arrangements to change a situation they don't like. After a while they encounter another unhappy situation with someone else. Feedback is given and life goes on. For some reason people get tangled up in unhappy situations that keep on repeating time after time. They keep looking for solutions outside themselves. It's always good to give feedback. But if it doesn't work, patterns keep on repeating.

In the eastern world, people don't give feedback. They adjust to their environment and lose who they really are. To adjust constantly to your environment uses a lot of energy and takes people from their life mission. It feels like being a puppet on a string. This also becomes a repeating pattern.

The way to break unwanted patterns is to live life according to Unity Conscious Leadership™.

2. Unity Conscious Leadership™; breaking obstructive patterns

Life according to Unity Conscious Leadership™ is a journey on our unique life path. During our journey we meet new people and encounter new situations. Some feel like a *warm bath*, and some 'trigger' us like an *obstacle* on our pathway.

It's a continuous process of lifelong learning by working on self-reflection, awareness and personal growth in the midst of society, and finding answers and the keys to solutions in ourselves.

The moments when obstacles arise are *learning* moments. The obstacle can be a person or a situation preventing you from achieving your goals. When you are in the middle of that kind of situation, it's hard to think about finding the solution in yourself.

If you encounter your obstacles as a mirror where you are observing yourself in a certain situation, you can reflect and ask yourself questions such as: what was I thinking, feeling, saying? And how did I act?

For example, if someone has an underlying fundamental feeling or belief of not being seen or heard, others tend to walk away and not listen, so it becomes a self-fulfilling prophecy.

When you become aware of this happening, ask yourself: Have I had these thoughts and feelings before? Have I used these words before? And did I act this way before? You might discover a pattern in your life. A pattern such as: feeling abandoned and neglected, having difficulty finding the place where you belong, making yourself smaller or bigger, feeling responsible for everyone, lacking the courage to ask for help, feelings of sadness or wanting to withdraw from society.

You can break through this pattern by finding appropriate professional guidance to help you see your way through obstructive patterns. The hidden potentials, gifts, qualities and life-giving energy will be released, and these will give you insights and bring you closer to your feeling of absolute happiness. A feeling of happiness you will radiate and share with everyone regardless of your situation.

And when you encounter another obstacle on your journey, do the same as before. *That's what they call lifelong learning.*

Summary

Dualism (Individualism and Collectivism)	**Unity Conscious Leadership™**
1. Person and environment are separated	1. Person and environment are one
2. Hierarchy and inequality	2. Equivalence without ranks and positions
3. Communicating in a language of opposites	3. Communicating in a language of oneness
4. Creating patterns and paradoxes	4. Breaking obstructive patterns
5. Feedback and looking for a solution outside	5. Self-reflection and growth
6. Learning by accident	6. Continuous process of lifelong learning

Patterns and Paradoxes

> *What makes the desert beautiful is*
> *that somewhere it hides a well.*
>
> – Antoine De Saint-Exupéry, The little Prince –

Patterns

> *Encounters generate triggers,*
> *triggers awaken memories,*
> *memories ignite emotions,*
> *emotions manifest feelings,*
> *feelings cause thoughts,*
> *thoughts become words,*
> *words become actions,*
> *actions create worlds.*
>
> – Joyce Z. Wazirali –

During my research with clients over 30 years about what it is that mostly moves people, I discovered that they get unconsciously triggered by a person or situation and as a result act in a certain way. Often it seemed that these triggers and reactions repeatedly occurred as a pattern in their lives.

The root cause of these triggers was mostly trauma they experienced in their own lives or inherited through the generations from their ancestors. By working on breaking through these patterns, revealing and integrating the 'locked potential' in the trauma, they transformed and their situations changed in a prosperous direction.

Patty

Patty came to my practice after she had burned-out. Over the course of one year, lying on her bed to get her energy back, she had sessions with a cognitive therapist. After one year she had enough energy to start working again. Within a week she was burned-out again.

During our introductory session, I realized Patty felt very responsible and was taking care of everyone, didn't dare to say 'no' or ask for help and didn't take time to charge her own battery. She was always busy with other people, which was why everyone came to her. When she helped others, she felt appreciated and people liked her. That was what she was unconsciously longing for all the time.

During the sessions with me, Patty realized she was doing the same things at her workplace as she had done at home since she was a little girl. It was a normal pattern in her life. When she was a little girl, her father worked hard. He came home when she was sleeping and left home before she woke up. Patty was the oldest child in the family. When her baby sister was born, she decided to take the place of her father, taking care and giving love to her baby sister and helping her mother at home.

We worked on her trauma of missing her father and his love, releasing the burdens she carried on her shoulders that didn't belong to her. It seemed to be that all the first-born women in the past generations showed the same pattern in their lives. The cause of the burnout was revealed.

As a result, Patty could sleep well, woke up vivid and energized, could ask for help, leave the responsibility of others to others, started to devote quality time to herself and discovered that she was a talented painter.

She went back to work. Her colleagues noticed that she wasn't taking responsibility for them anymore. Many years passed and the burnout never came back.

A. Roots of Patterns

People develop patterns of behavior intrinsic drivers of which they are mostly unconscious. In contact with the outside world, the intrinsic drivers ignite and people think, feel and behave in a particular way, such as *thinking that other people are better then they themselves are, feeling small, being unable to show their full potential.*

It is striking that there are many intrinsic drivers. Depending on the encounter or situation, certain drivers are triggered and ignite.

Thoughts, feelings and actions will unconsciously arise. Depending on the occasion a different combination of inner drivers may arise.

Patterns have their origin in dualism. In my opinion and experience with my clients, the patterns develop after an event that was experienced as traumatic created a spin-off from an original state of oneness. The very first event had taken place so long ago that people do not remember it and do not know how it originated, so attempts are made to resolve these patterns from the perspective of dualism. As a result, the patterns increase and are further reinforced.

B. Trauma and Hidden Potential

A trauma is a very severe shock or an extremely upsetting experience, which may cause psychological or physical damage.

You can see a trauma in the example of an oyster that starts to excrete material that becomes mother-of-pearl through the irritation of a penetrated grain of sand. As a result, the irritation starts to grow. Meanwhile, the oyster is increasingly secreting mother-of-pearl. In the end, the grain of sand has become a beautiful pearl.

Roots of patterns are mostly coming from a traumatic experience. For generations, the traumatic experience stays in the collective memory of the person until it's discovered and resolved.

From my experience with trauma processing, I have noticed that trauma also isolates potential at the same time. Processing the trauma and integrating the isolated potential creates growth and releases emotional strength.

C. Examples of Trauma on Personal Level

Here are some examples of personal trauma: an undesired birth, miscarriage, abortion, missing of family members, denial of existence of a family member, excluding of family members, secrets, emigration, adoption, divorce, alcohol and/ or drug addiction, war and other extreme event, death of a loved one, death in childbirth, unfair division of inheritance, children taking care of their parents at a young age, children giving love to their parents in an unbalanced way, staying in a boarding school, prison or hospital.

We don't have to experience the trauma ourselves. We also inherit traumas from our ancestors on an unconscious level which influence our lives and behaviour in the here and now.

D. Examples of Patterns and *Behaviour* on Personal Level

- Feeling abandoned, *closing off from one's environment*
- Feeling neglected, *wanting to belong somewhere*
- Having a hard time recognizing your own place, *searching for your own place in life or never feeling at home*
- Feeling unheard or unseen, *ending up in situations of being neglected*

- Feeling smaller than others, *looking up to other people*
- Feeling bigger than others, *presenting yourself as better than others*
- Feeling responsible for everyone, *always ready to help others or not daring to say no*
- Lacking the courage to ask for help, *not daring to ask for help*
- Sadness, *crying quickly*
- Withdrawing from society, *not showing up at an appointment*
- Feeling emptiness inside, *seeking appreciation and confirmation from others or becoming addicted*
- A feeling of not being loved, *always asking for or wanting love from others*
- Anxiety in many forms, *afraid of some people or situations*
- Always in the head and thinking a lot, *thinking and talking a lot*
- Can't get in touch with feelings, *lost connection with own feelings or missing empathy*
- Medically inexplicable physical complaints, *complaining a lot about inexplicable pain*

Paradoxes

Paradoxes are patterns with contradicting dynamics, such as: inclusion and exclusion, trust and distrust, victim and perpetrator. These dynamics keeps perpetuating, and they occur between individuals and within organizations and systems.

Paradoxes appear when a group of people are united with a common aim. It can be at the workplace, sports place, with friends, family gatherings, at school, in the schoolyard, etcetera.

Suicide of a colleague and a dear friend

Lenny was working at a company where she met her colleague, Chris. Lenny and Chris started a very dear friendship. They were both married.

Chris had three young children.

At some point, Lenny noticed that Chris was living a luxurious life he simply could not afford with the salary he earned from the company. Because of his luxurious life, he had a lot of friends.

One day Lenny discovered that Chris had been committing fraud for a while. Because of the fraud the company would go bankrupt and not only Lenny but all her colleagues would lose their job, including Chris. Lenny realized she had to stop Chris and confronted him with her discovery. The next day Lenny decided she would tell the director about her discovery. It was a difficult decision for her because she and Chris were good friends. Chris and his family felt as though they were a part of Lenny's family. Chris would get fired, it would be the end of their relationship and he would experience financial problems.

The morning Lenny had planned to tell her boss about the fraud, Chris' wife called her to tell her that Chris had committed suicide, leaving a note for his family and his boss with an explanation of his fraud.

One year after this happened, Lenny came to me. Every day when she went to the office a feeling of guilt about the suicide of Chris came over her. She couldn't talk to anyone at the company about it, because they could accuse her of being complicit in the fraud. As a result, she could not concentrate on her job and had unexplainable physical and mental complaints.

Lenny couldn't live with that secret and shared it with me. We worked on the traumatic event which had gone on to affect her day and night.

After we worked together, Lenny's feeling of guilt was gone and never reappeared. She could concentrate again and the unexplained physical and mental complaints vanished.

A. Roots of Paradoxes

Like patterns, paradoxes have their origin in dualism. In my opinion and experiences with my clients, the paradoxes are a spin-off from an original oneness caused by an event that was experienced as traumatic. The very first event took place so long ago that people do not know how it originated. Attempts are made to resolve these paradoxes from the perspective of dualism. As a result, the paradoxes increase and are further reinforced.

B. The Occurrence of Undercurrent

The paradoxes as a dynamic in an organization are extremely complex. On the one hand we have the collective memory of the organization keeping all traumas from the past in the system, manifesting patterns and paradoxes. On the other hand, all the staff take their personal collective memory of patterns and paradoxes into the organization. The mix of the collective memory of the organization and the people within, produces a chemical reaction which is called *the undercurrent*.

C. Examples of Trauma on Organisational Level

Examples of trauma on an organisational level might include unjustified dismissal, succession within a (family) company, merger, reorganization, non-recognition of a founder, power and influence structures, damaged trust, affective relationships between superiors and subordinates, a formal leader who could not tolerate or fulfill his leadership responsibility, struggles or lack of cooperation between different departments and subgroups, survival of old pain and historical obstructions, lack of clarity about responsibilities, overall need for decisiveness, and accidents suffered by staff members at the workplace.

D. Examples of Paradoxes and *Behaviour* in Organizations

(also called the Dynamic or undercurrent in the Culture)

- Inclusion and exclusion, *People get the feeling they either belong or do not belong to a group*
- Thoughts directed inwards and outwards, *one group is busy only with what's happening in the system and the other group is focussed on what's going on outside the system*
- Power and powerlessness, *People have a sense of strength and weakness at the same time*
- Trust and distrust, *there is trust and suspicion running alongside each other*
- Flexibility and inflexibility, People *want to change but are reluctant to take the necessary steps*
- Division and togetherness, *some people feel alone and others are with a clique within the group*
- Accelerate and brake, *taking steps forward and suddenly being forced to stop*
- Us and them, *talking about 'us' as one entity, and 'them' as a second entity*
- Dependence and independence, *waiting for each other to act, and acting without taking account of the others*
- Giving space and taking space, *by giving others the opportunity to act while taking the opportunity to act independently*
- In contact and out of contact, *being connected to each other superficially but not being with each other*

- Responsible and irresponsible, *taking or claiming the responsibility whilst at the same moment not taking responsibility*
- Attraction and repulsion, *to like and dislike at the same time, to have mixed feelings about*
- Victim and perpetrator, *one is suffering while the other causes the suffering*

Breaking Through Patterns and Paradoxes

> *To me, you are nothing more than a little boy who is just like a hundred thousand other little boys.*
> *And I have no need of you.*
> *And to you, I am nothing more than a fox like a hundred thousand other foxes.*
> *But if you tame me, then we shall need each other.*
> *To me, you will be unique in all the world.*
> *To you, I shall be unique in all the world.*
>
> – Antoine de Saint-Exupéry, The Little Prince –

Three Stages in Character Development

> *'The living secret of life is always hidden between two people, and this is the true mystery that words cannot betray and arguments cannot exhaust.'*
>
> – Carl Gustav Jung –

A. From the perspective of *dualism*

<u>Dependent or co-dependent relationship</u> is an approach which implies a deal between the parties to exchange with each other. Such as, ***I will love you if you give me what I need***, or ***I will stay with you as long as you take care of me.***

<u>Independent relationship</u> - standing alone and happy: 'I am in a control state, I have everything I need to make me happy.'

B. From the perspective of Unity Conscious Leadership™

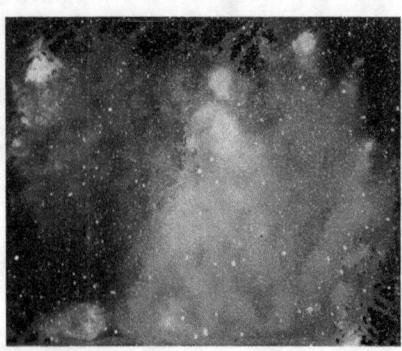

<u>Interdependent relationships</u>, seeing your outer world as a reflection of your inner world, using obstructive relationships for inner transformation and growth.

The Chinese character for this concept depicts transformation occurring in the space between people. **Transformation is the result of interacting with others with the intention of fostering *mutual* growth.** Our growth is an interdependent process and is also the ***key point of the Lotus Sutra***.

While we enter relationships, it is important to view all of them as fertile ground for growth, development, maturation and strengthening of our own character. The **self-actualization** (*expressing the need* to make optimum use of opportunities to get the best out of ourselves) that we undergo in a good relationship is what makes us happy, rather than the relationship itself. This kind of growth and emotional development is termed **human revolution**. An inner transformation.

The *Lens* of Unity Conscious Leadership™

The origin of patterns and paradoxes can be traced back to individualism and collectivism, both of which I believe originated from the paradigm of *dualism*. Leadership from the perspective of dualism creates more of the same and new patterns and paradoxes.

Unity Conscious Leadership™, which assumes that everything comes from one source and that everyone and all things are interconnected and influence each other, is the paradigm in which patterns and paradoxes can be broken.

The way to become aware and break through obstructive patterns and paradoxes is through the perspective of interdependency in relationships and situations.

The Lotus Sutra, explains the complex interdependence of life. The "lens" of Unity Conscious Leadership™, will help you lift the veils and discover some secrets of the Lotus Sutra that will help you transform in an easy way.

Human revolution

Human revolution is a state of life and awareness of obstructing triggers occurring at moments of interdependency. It involves discovering obstructing patterns in your life through self-reflection and breaking through these patterns by growth and emotional development with the help of a professional coach, counsellor or therapist.

Patterns expand unconsciously

Personal layer

If someone experiences a particular pattern in life, such as feeling abandoned, for some reason the person encounters situations in his life where he feels that nobody likes him and no one wants to connect with him.

In an organization or workplace, the same person experiences a paradox of inclusion and exclusion. In this case, he has the feeling of being excluded while others are included.

Jennifer

Jennifer was a vivid, playful and creative girl who was bullied at her primary school. As a result, she became withdrawn and lacked the confidence to do anything and isolated herself as a result. She came to me when she was at secondary school and feeling depressed, being angry with anyone who approached her. Thus, she had only one friend.

By processing the trauma of the bullying, the isolated potential was released. She became vivid and playful again, motivated, happy, made more friends and regained her inner motivation to work for her future.

Organizational layer

Patterns displayed by leaders in organizations unconsciously influence the individuals and the organization dynamic. The people in the organization show behaviour which is not normal for them. They feel as though there is an undercurrent.

Fighting at the schoolyard

There was a school with two departments - Dutch and English. During the break times, there were regular conflicts and fights between the Dutch-speaking children and the English speakers. There was a pattern of inclusion and exclusion, 'us against you' or 'the Dutch against the English'. I was wondering why they split into two groups and started to fight with each other. Children should make friends and play with each other. In this case, they didn't even know each other.

I finally understood what was really happening when a teacher told me that it was difficult to get the *teachers* from the two departments working together. They were two separate 'camps'. Only two or three teachers were in contact with both departments. While the two camps shared one teachers' room where they all met during the break, the two groups avoided contact with each other. They were literally standing apart from each other.

Then of course, I realized that the children on the playground were merely reflecting what was going on between the teachers: a dynamic on a different layer within the organization which they could not see but could sense unconsciously.

Only one half of the staff got sick after a staff party

One Monday morning I met the school director in the hallway. She looked rather worried. I asked her how she was doing. She said she was doing well personally, but the previous Saturday they had held a staff party. On the Monday morning, twenty of the forty employees reported sick. She said she did not understand why so many people were at home with abdominal pain. Everyone had eaten the same food. The other half of the staff came to work and had no complaints.

I told her, 'the people who had reported sick possibly felt that something substantial was about to change in the school in the short term and had yet to be announced, or it had only just been announced.' 'That could be possible ' she said, and walked on.

A few weeks later, she announced she was to leave the organization due to a new job elsewhere. During the staff party she had already made the decision but kept it to herself. Unconsciously several of her staff members felt that something radical was going to happen that made them feel unwell.

Conclusion

Obstructing patterns and paradoxes occur and multiply on multiple layers in life when we perceive our world from the perspective of *dualism,* creating more separateness and contradiction in the world.

By observing our world through the lens of Unity Conscious Leadership™, veils will be lifted and some of life's secrets will be revealed that will help us transform in an easy way. As a result, more unity and thus, more health, happiness and peace will be brought into the world.

CHAPTER 2

INTERDEPENDENT GROWTH AND TRANSFORMATION

*It is much more difficult to judge oneself
than to judge others.
If you succeed in judging yourself rightly,
then you are indeed a man of true wisdom.*

– Antoine de Saint-Exupéry, The Little Prince –

Triggers are the Keys to Transformation

*Our encounter with life is currently taking place.
And the meeting place is exactly in the here and now.*

- Buddha -

Wherever we are, or whatever we think right now, represents our experience in the *here and now*. This place is full of triggers which unconsciously influence our state of life. From my own experience and according to the Lotus Sutra, the following dynamic of three principles arise:

1. Unity of person and environment,

2. The law of cause and effect, and
3. The all-pervasive influence of the past, present and future in the *here and now*.

The symbol of Unity Consciousness is often presented as a lemniscate, the shape of a sideways figure of eight. Meaning people and environment are interconnected with each other through infinity of cause and effect and the three existent periods of past, present and future.

The dynamic of the three principles

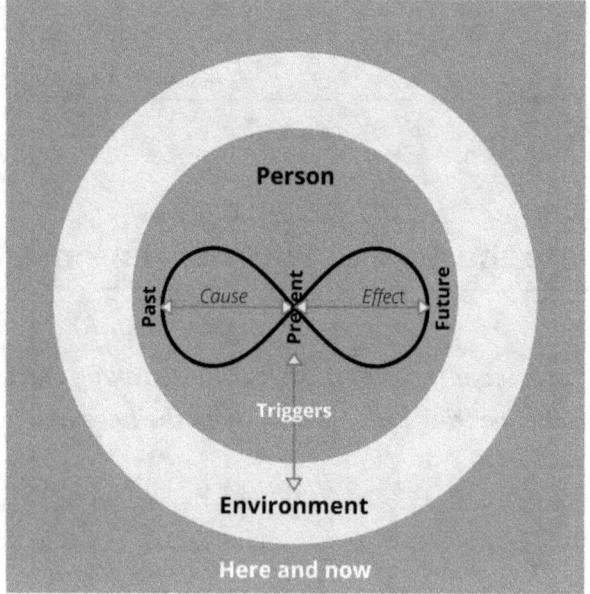

Francis

Francis has been a medical professional for decades. His overall passion is to help his patients. But on the other hand, he has known resistance to the healer in himself. For instance, on occasion, he finds himself working with patients by pushing the gas pedal while at the same time, easing up a little.

His talent as a healer was especially important for him. This was why he wanted to know why there was also resistance and where it came from.

The experience of the resistance gave him a feeling of fear, sadness, powerlessness, dependence and being unseen.

His first memory of this kind of feeling was when he was around five. He was living in France, and his tonsils had to be taken out. It felt at the time as though his own will and needs were not important. He was afraid and had to stay a day and a night at the hospital without his parents. As a result, he felt abandoned and distressed. The nurses were kind, but it seemed that the doctors did not see him and thought that he was not important.

When he moved to the Netherlands with his parents, he didn't dare to stay alone anywhere. Separation anxiety made him afraid of going to parties, swimming competitions, school outings, sleep parties and camp. He also had a fear of abandonment, afraid that if his parents left, they would not come back.

The previous year at the age of 45, he had been to France for a therapy session. Initially he stayed in a hotel that was an old French spa. He felt unhappy there and thought that if he stayed there, he would lose control. So, he checked out. After discussing this, he realized that the rooms and corridors must have reminded him strongly of his experience at the hospital when he was young.

Together, we did an intervention to enable him to cope with the trauma of his youth.

During the intervention Francis felt and became aware of specific physical tension at the height of his left back region and neck. These physical feelings he knew very well. They occurred when he was very scared, nervous or stressed about something.

He forgave the nurses, doctors, his parents, sisters, brother and also himself, following which the tension in his neck and head region disappeared.

He also released the potential he had lost in the trauma. The potential of feeling safe and loved, able to be alone without feeling abandoned.

The resistance he had towards his profession as a healer is also now gone. Rather, he feels truly passionate about what he does.

Unity of Person and Environment

*Unity conscious living is like
looking to your environment
as if
you're looking in your mirror.*

– Albert Einstein –

'Be the change you want to see in the world', 'be the hero you want to see in the world',

'every other is a mirror for me', are well-known inspirational quotes. The question is, how do you take this approach? What are you going to change?

It starts with becoming aware of wanting to change certain things in your life. How can a change in *you* change your environment? The answer is through Unity Conscious Leadership™.

My mirrors at home

One day I was preparing dinner in the kitchen while my kids (5 and 2 years old) were sitting far away from each other at the dinner table. Suddenly I heard both crying loudly. I thought something terrible must have happened. When I ran to them, they were sitting on their chairs at a distance from each other, so they could not have hurt each other. When I asked my son (the oldest) what happened, he answered: *'It's your sadness mom! We can feel your sadness.'*

They made me realise I was sad without being aware of it. At that time, I stopped feeling for a while. I immediately took action to work on my mood to lift the burdens from my children's shoulders.

My mirrors in the organization

As co-founder and director of a company grown from two founders to 80 staff members in 13 years, I was aware that my state of mind had a direct effect on the staff.

On days when I was insufficiently rested, I noticed that the employees were delayed and less productive. Or if I had a sad day, which they could not see on the outside, the employees were more emotional.

Thanks to the courses I followed in the field of personal development, I worked on my own personal development and noticed that it not only had an effect on myself, but also on our staff members.

The Law of Cause and Effect

What makes the leaves of trees move?
What makes waves come and go?
What makes water move?
Who or what determines the direction of the movement?
Visible effects are often driven by invisible causes.

– Joyce Z. Wazirali –

The reality of our daily lives is based on the operation of the *'law of cause and effect'* that encompasses past, present and future. Every moment we create a latent, invisible cause with everything we think, say and do. When activated by an external incentive, it manifests itself as a consequence, the events and experiences in our daily lives. Our response to this again causes more latent, invisible causes: a continuous cycle that forms our subjective life experience.

Because no living creature is independent of its environment, the consequences will also become visible in the environment. The word "environment" here does not mean a general environment in which life takes place. But it points to the unique circumstances of every living creature in which its individual patterns appear. In other words, a living being and its environment are one and inseparable. According to Buddhism, everything around us, including our work and family relationships, is the reflection of our inner life. Everything is perceived by the "self" and changes with our state of life. So, if we change our state of life, our situation will also change.

Interdependent Growth and Transformation

In Buddhism, the lotus flower symbolizes our lives. The lotus is a beautiful flower that floats on the surface of the water, and its roots growing in the mud nourish its beauty. The mud is symbolic of the difficulties in life through which the Lotus flower grows. This plant carries flowers and seeds at the same time. If one compares the flower with the cause and the fruits with the effect, the lotus symbolizes the way in which cause and effect are present in life at the same time, in the here and now.

Shakyamuni Buddha revealed in the "Law of the Lotus" that the simultaneity of cause and effect allows us to bring out the infinite capacities that we possess in our lives and to achieve a state of complete freedom that reaches the three periods of existence: past, present and future. How do we do that? Through a change deep within our own heart or mind, we express our absolute happiness directly in our lives, here and now.

We are used to watching television and tuning into several channels to see a movie, sports, a documentary or whatever we are in the mood for, without thinking about how it works.

We can see the frequency waves we use to tune in to receive a channel as the cause. The effect is what we see on the screen. We need the television as a tool to transform the invisible cause (frequency waves) into a visible effect (what we see on the screen).

The television represents our lives and who we are at this moment. If you want to change the effects in your life, or what happens in your environment, you should work on the (invisible) cause or the frequency waves you are receiving with your senses (along with your past memories and future expectations). The tool to see the cause and effect in your life is the lens of Unity Conscious Leadership™.

The All-Pervasive Influence of the Past, Present and Future

What kinds of causes am I making right now?
What actions am I taking?
The answers to these questions are what will determine our future.

– Daisaku Ikeda[3] –

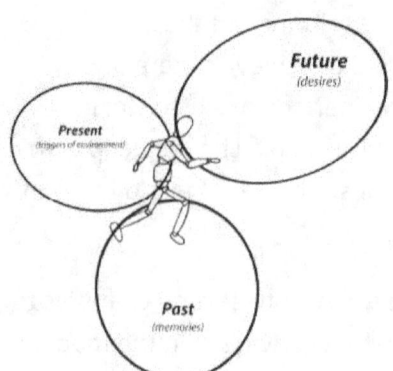

We all (including the rivers, mountains and sand grains) are creatures and creators of this planet and Universe. We are interconnected, interdependent and influencing each other (un)consciously all the time.

Our past, present and future are intertwined like a garment we weave together to create one whole, while the mystical Law of visible and invisible cause and effect paints patterns in our garment. Those patterns can sometimes result in weaving errors, errors which originate in invisible (tragic) events from the past, becoming visible as a consequence of something in the present.

---

[3] Daisaku Ikeda (born on January 2nd 1928 in Tokyo) is a peace builder, Buddhist philosopher, educator, author and poet. As third president of the Soka Gakkai lay Buddhist organization in Japan, founding president of the Soka Gakkai International (SGI) and founder of several international institutions promoting peace, culture and education, he has dedicated himself to bolstering the foundations of a lasting culture of peace.
A core focus of Ikeda's peace activities has been the goal of nuclear disarmament. As leader of the SGI, he has inspired grassroots efforts for a nuclear-weapons-free world over several decades and has continued to explore viable routes toward nuclear abolition in his peace proposals, published annually since 1983.

An experience with a client

Some years ago, I had a client. She was 50 years old and mother of three adult children. She was always worrying about her son. It was as if though he was still a toddler who was not able to take responsibility for his own life. *Her desire* was that one day he would stand on his own feet, which had not happened for some reason. For many years she went on to control and guide him until one day she was burned-out.

During our session, she realized that her parents were still treating her as if she was a toddler. Even at the age of 50. It became clear to her that there were patterns for generations where the parents saw their children as toddlers even when they were adults. The cause of these patterns originated from a traumatic experience affecting her parents and herself. Her parents divorced when she was a toddler and she divorced from the father of her children when her son was a toddler. Breaking through this pattern released not only my client from the ancestral burden, but also her adult son to stand on his own feet and take responsibility for himself. Since our session, without knowing about anything about the session, her son started to take responsibility. My client doesn't have to worry about him anymore. She enjoys his company and feels more energized.

The dynamic of time in the here and now, and through generations

The here and now is where the past, present and future manifest simultaneously and combine to create the dynamic of the here and now. That is how subconscious *memories* from the past, *desires* for the future and the present *environment* combine to create triggers from inside. Therefore, people often feel pulled in all directions, get stuck, cannot make choices or perhaps make random choices, the outcome of which they cannot know. So, it becomes a matter of trial and error.

Inheriting the dynamic through generations

Besides through our own life experiences, we also unconsciously inherit the dynamic (which manifests as patterns) from our ancestors, influencing us in the here and now. It is as though we are living their lives. By working on breaking through these patterns, in a short time, my clients experienced a major durable positive change.

Desires are opportunities for growth

Sometimes someone longs for or craves certain feelings, perhaps because they lost them somewhere in the past due to life experiences, a trauma perhaps. A child who is traumatized at a young age and suddenly takes on an adult position, loses its innocence, and feelings of safety and being loved. They can also lose their creativity, playfulness, and entrepreneurial spirit. Everything that made that child *be a child* would be lost in the trauma. However, there is still hope because *those qualities are still there.* A desire may lie in the future, but the solution is still in the past. That is how and why past, present and future are intertwined in the here and now.

The shadow side of desires

Sometimes people can express their desires in certain behaviour or actions such as jealousy, envy, slander, bullying, stealing and so on. Behind these actions are feelings of discontent or *resentful longing* aroused by someone else's possessions, qualities or luck. They project their desires onto other people. By investigating the *root cause* of their desires and solving it, their behaviour can change.

The Power of Forgiveness; *Turning Poison into Medicine*

> **Forgive others,**
> **not because they deserve forgiveness,**
> **but because you deserve peace.**
>
> – Jonathan Lockwood Huie –

Immaculée Ilibagiza

Immaculée Ilibagiza born in Rwanda in 1972, is a Roman Catholic writer and speaker from Rwanda. She is Tutsi, so she had to go into hiding during the 1994 Rwandan genocide. During that time, she survived for three months with seven other women in a bathroom measuring 0.91 x 1.20 m. During those three months they suffered from hunger, thirst, anger and pain. The pastor, a man from the Hutu tribe (their enemy) saved their lives and gave them a bible so they could pray.

Immaculée couldn't say the words *'forgive us the trespass as we forgive those'*. She skipped that part of the prayer because, she thought; *we* didn't do anything wrong; *we* are the *victims* and they are the *perpetrators*. That made her feel better. Then suddenly her inner voice asked her: where do you want to stand? With love, or with hate? She thought of the people who stand for love such as Nelson Mandela, Mother Theresa and Mahatma Gandhi. Then she thought of people who stand for hate, such as Adolf Hitler. She opted for love and a shift in her happened and changed everything. She felt love, and compassion for the perpetrators. She asked herself what would happen if one day the perpetrators woke up and realized what they had done. They killed her mother, father, two brothers, grandmother, grandfather and school friends.

She could see where evil and hate can take people to.

After the war she visited the prison to see the man who killed her mother and brother. He was a man she knew - her schoolteacher. He had been like a father to her, she had eaten lunch with his family. She cried out of compassion for him and his family; '*I forgive you!*' she said. She wanted him to be free of her. Making his own journey *from his heart*. Not from anger.

At the darkest hours of her life, Immaculée Ilibagiza chose love instead of hate. She chose to belong to the group of people who are examples to the world when it comes to personal leadership and forgiveness.

You don't have to choose someone so famous. It can also be a neighbour or someone you have met in your daily life. To forgive is sometimes exceedingly difficult. How can you forgive someone who crossed your boundaries?

Forgiving is not easy - but forgiving is...

- Making yourself free, growing wings to go on with your future
- Freeing yourself of the negative energy blocks you're carrying
- Something you can only do from your heart
- Looking at the other from your heart and seeing the innocence through the behaviour of the other person
- Making miracles possible
- Out of love for yourself
- Letting go the hope for a better past
- Turning poison into medicine
- Freeing yourself from something you are expecting from someone else
- Forgiving yourself even if you don't know why
- Getting your strength and life-giving energy back

Nelson Mandela's way to forgive

As Nelson Mandela left prison, he said: *as I stand before the door to my freedom, I realise that if I do not leave my pain, anger and bitterness behind me, I will still be in prison.*

Self-imprisonment is worse than that imposed. How many of us have imprisoned ourselves inside walls of anger and bitterness, holding grudges, etcetera? Forgiveness sets you free. Get out of your prison.

If you want to forgive someone to unburden your future life, even if the other person has passed away, go to a professional who can help you. There are several ways to forgive. It depends upon what suits you.

What if one day you realize that you are a perpetrator?

In my practice I also guide clients who have hurt other people in the past and realized what they did. People who were bullying others at the schoolyard, at home or even at the workplace. It makes me happy if people become aware of what they caused in the past and are yearning to make amends for the sake of their future and that of others.

During the time at the Plasa Group, we had a client who was always grumpy and complaining about our staff. After a while, the staff went into hiding when he arrived at the office. They had to prepare themselves for his grumpy behaviour. He was the only client who behaved this way, so the staff knew they were not to blame.

One day our grumpy client was diagnosed with cancer and given just a few weeks to live. That was the moment in his life he looked back at his past and thought about his loved ones who had already passed away. He realized that from his childhood on, he missed the love of his parents who were always grumpy with him and whatever he did, it was never right. When he thought about how he treated the people in his environment, he realized his behaviour was reflecting that of his parents towards him. The moment of regret came when he was weak and waiting for death.

He used his final remaining energy to apologize to our staff for how he had treated them. Unconsciously he projected his pain onto his environment and the people who were useful to him. His gesture dissolved the tension that was always there when he came.

It takes courage to admit guilt if you realize that you have hurt other people in the past.

Projection is Perception

The world is in the eye of the beholder.

– Lotus Sutra –

Not forgiving is the commitment to keep connected to the pain, guilt or regret that more empathic people are carrying in their daily lives, which consciously and subconsciously influences their thoughts, the words they use and the actions they take in life. Every day, without noticing, people project their pain, guilt and regret onto their environment. They even pass it subconsciously through to the next generation.

Meanwhile, they will experience situations that remind them of the pain they are carrying with them. People will react to situations as they could not perhaps react to that original event or to the person who had hurt them at the time.

Triggers

I remember, during an evaluation interview with an external agency telling the director of the organization when asked if we needed a projector: *that is not necessary because we are already projecting on each other all day long.* My answer came spontaneously, and he looked at me and smiled.

We are often not aware of it. And it happens so fast that we don't even notice it. We can be unknowingly triggered by someone's appearance, what the person says or how he behaves. The trigger was once a small seed in the past that has started to sprout and grow unconsciously over the years. And every external trigger awakens our unconscious memories of that seed that we once planted and hid somewhere far away. We even forget those seeds of our own past and those inherited from our ancestors.

For example,

At one point, a client asked me how he might best deal with his aversion to his future executives, following structural changes in the organization for which he worked. For many years, he had been a manager and having built up a great team, he really enjoyed his job.

His fear was that he would lose the responsibility he currently enjoyed, and from which he gained so much energy and satisfaction.

He had already met his future executives and felt averse to cooperating with them. Even meeting them made him tense.

He had a pleasant relationship with his current colleagues, as well as a permanent contract and good salary. Departing was not an option for him. What he needed was to look at his future executives in a different way. He asked me how he could achieve that.

When I asked him how he saw his future supervisors, he said that one was quite aggressive and narcissistic and the other came across as a small child.

I asked about his home situation when he lived at home with his parents. My question surprised him. He had come to me with a question about his work situation and I started by asking questions about his home situation. He did not understand the connection.

When I said I look at people and their environment more broadly, to better help them, he relaxed and started to tell me about his childhood.

He was the oldest child in the family, and he found himself standing between his parents at a young age. Because his father was aggressive and had narcissistic traits, my client wanted to protect his mother because he saw her as vulnerable. As a result, he caught his father's fist which was intended for his mother.

I suggested he go back to his thoughts and feelings about his future executives, to see what he noticed.

He was immediately aware that he projected his past situation onto his future executives. Then other situations from his past emerged, which in retrospect were all his projections from his childhood trauma.

It was a pattern in his life. Whenever he had contact with elderly people, he became tense but didn't know why. I guided him through the processing of his childhood trauma, so that he could take responsibility for his own life and leave the responsibility of others to others.

The merger at his workplace became a fact and his new executives turned out to be great people. The change had taken place within him. The projection of his childhood trauma was removed. And without thinking, he could see his executives from a pure perspective. That made him more relaxed at work and meant he could continue in the job without stress.

The Coherence and Alchemy of Life....

A. From a Buddhist Perspective: Eastern Wisdom

Many people experience their life and environment as two separate things that are completely separate from each other. But from the all-embracing vision of Buddhist philosophy, they are one, and inseparably linked. We often tend to blame circumstances and others for our problems and suffering. However, the principle "unity of person and environment" shows that the cause of our joy and sorrow lies in ourselves. When we base ourselves on this and consider our environment as a mirror of our inner life, we can take responsibility for our lives, solve our problems, and change our circumstances for the better.

Our outlook on life and our questions about our existence stem from our 'self' consciousness. We believe that our 'self' is the basis of reality and we look at everything else in relation to our 'self'. This means that we do not see life as a *whole* but that everything is separate: the 'self' and others, internal and external, body and mind, spiritual and material, human and nature. Buddhism teaches us that the 'self' is only a temporary phenomenon: a *temporary combination* of the physical and spiritual body and mind.

The principle of 'unity of person and environment' makes it clear that we can influence and improve our environment through an inner change or by raising our consciousness or state of life. It teaches us that our state of life is expressed in our environment. When we experience depression, this is reflected in the way we respond to events and in our environment. When we are full of joy, this will also be reflected in our environment. If our state of life is compassion, we will experience protection and support from our environment. By increasing our state of life, we can change our environment.

Everything is interconnected, and our lives exert a deep boundless influence. The more we are aware of our great power *and use it*, and the more we believe that our actions can make a difference, *the more we can actually be the change we want to see in the world.*

Lotus Sutra

In the Lotus Sutra, the historical Buddha Shakyamuni announced 2,600 years ago the existence of innumerable galaxies and the possibility of sentient life on planets outside our own. This was without the aid of telescopes, high technology or even the written word. The Buddhist model strongly resembles the cosmology accepted today. The Buddha postulated a cosmos that is theoretically consistent with what many scientists now propose. In fundamental ways, Buddhist theory accepts the vast dimensions and space-time concepts of modern physics and is even congruent with the more abstruse realm of quantum theory. It contains a detailed analysis of life that penetrates the depth of the human psyche. Buddhism is a driving force that enables individual human beings to bring about their own spiritual reformation, thereby assuring eternal peace and the long-term survival of civilizations.

B. From a Scientific Perspective; Western Knowledge

> *If there is any religion that could cope with modern scientific needs, it would be Buddhism.*
>
> – Albert Einstein –

Albert Einstein

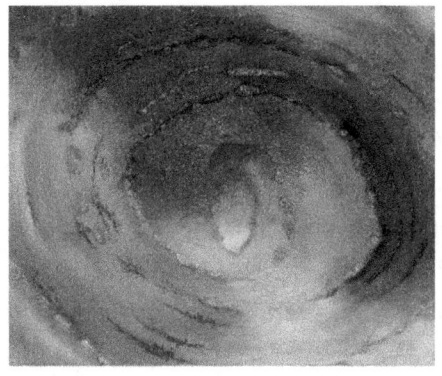

According to Albert Einstein, a human being is a part of a whole, called by us a 'universe', a part limited in time and space. He experiences himself, his thoughts, and his and feelings as something separated from the rest. A kind of optical delusion of his consciousness. This delusion is a kind of prison for us, restricting us to our personal desires and to affection for a few persons nearest to us. Our task must be to free ourselves from this prison by widening our circle of compassion to embrace all living creatures and the whole of nature in its beauty.

David Bohm

What is needed in a relativistic theory is to give up altogether the notion that the world is constituted of basic objects or 'building blocks'. Rather one has to view the world in terms of universal flux of events and processes.

– David Bohm –

David Bohm (1917 -1992), was a theoretic physicist. During the early 1980s, in his book 'Wholeness and the Implicated Order', he developed a theory of quantum physics which treats the totality of existence as an unbroken whole. Bohm's main concern was with understanding the nature of reality in general and of consciousness in particular.

Consciousness (which we take to include thoughts, feelings, desires, will, and so on) is to be comprehended in terms of the *implicate order*, along with reality as a whole. The implicate order (also referred to as the *"enfolded"*) is seen as a deeper and more fundamental order of reality.

In contrast, the *explicate order* (also referred to as the *"unfolded"*) include the abstractions that humans normally perceive. As Bohm wrote, in the enfolded [or implicate] order, space and time are no longer the dominant factors determining the relationships of dependence or independence of different elements. Rather, an entirely different sort of basic connection of elements is possible, from which our ordinary notions of space and time, along with those of separately existent material particles, are abstracted as forms derived from the deeper order. These ordinary notions in fact appear in what is called the *"explicate" or "unfolded" order*, which is a special and distinguished form contained within the general totality of all the implicate orders (Bohm 1980, p. xv).

Carl Gustav Jung

> *There is no coming to consciousness without pain,*
> *People will do anything, no matter how absurd,*
> *in order to avoid facing their own soul.*
> *One does not become enlightened by imagining figures of light,*
> *but by making the darkness conscious.*
>
> – Carl Gustav Jung –

Carl Gustav Jung teaches that, Collective Unconsciousness [4] and Collective Consciousness confront Personal Unconsciousness and Personal Consciousness.

---

[4] Unconscious means 'not awake' or 'lacking awareness'.
Subconscious refers to thoughts, actions or brain processes of which a person is not directly aware.

The Collective Unconsciousness is an ocean of primordial images and instincts which all people have in common.

The Personal Unconsciousness contains the Collective Unconsciousness, and is also a sum of all Unconsciousness contents that are related to an individual. This differs from person to person. These are experiences, feelings and facts you once were aware of but forgot or had never thought about. There may also be things that you have observed with your senses but that have not been picked up by your consciousness. Furthermore, there are deliberately repressed, imaginative representations, impressions and inclinations that you reject because you do not want to acknowledge under any circumstances, either for yourself or for another. You would rather deny them. They are your personal shadow parts. The personal unconscious.

The personal unconscious is in principle recognizable and forms an intriguing component of your personality. This is why it makes sense to become aware of it. The awareness is a part of the major work in your own individuation process. You will become personally conscious.
The more people become personally aware by healing themselves, the deeper the self-healing character of the human being will penetrate in the collective consciousness of a circle, community and the world. Everyone contributes. That is different from thinking that the world revolves around you. It's all about us, including you. Everyone is a star.

Rupert Sheldrake's concept of the Morphogenetic Fields

This concept illustrates the working of morphogenetic fields. Rupert Sheldrake (28 June 1942) is an English author who has further developed the concept of morphic field (based on the older concept of morphogenetic field: an energy-like field that defined the entire biology of all living beings). Sheldrake studied natural sciences and philosophy. From 1967 to 1973 he worked as a researcher and director of biochemistry and cell biology at the University of Cambridge. He has researched and written on topics including the development and behaviour of animals and plants, telepathy, perception and metaphysics. He has studied issues for which we do not yet have an explanation. Examples include the behaviour and mutual communication of ants, homing pigeons that find their loft, dogs that "know" when their owners return home, and more.

Morphogenesis stands for genesis (Genesis) of the form (Greek morphe), and is as complicated as the question: What came first, the chicken or the egg? The term 'Morphogenetic fields' literally means *fields that bring shape*. Sheldrake argues that natural systems at all levels, such as atoms, crystals, cells, tissues, organs and organisms, are inspired, organized and coordinated by morphic fields that contain an inherent memory.

Natural systems inherit this collective memory of all prior manifestations of their kind through morphic resonance, with the result that the patterns of development and behaviour become increasingly habitual through repetition. Rupert Sheldrake assumes the existence of those fields as a *genetic blueprint for every species on earth*. They penetrate the field of thought of every kind and determine every aspect of its evolution.

Zero Point Field and Quantum physics

Here I cite **Lynne McTaggert**,[5] international lecturer and author of the bestselling book *The Field* [6]; *'We are all connected by an energy field. We*

---

[5] (You tube: Lynne McTaggert on Quantum Physics 1 of 2)
[6] In this groundbreaking classic, Lynne reveals a radical new paradigm – that the human mind and body are not separate from their environment but a pocket of pulsating power constantly interacting with this vast energy sea, and that consciousness may be central in shaping our world.

swim in a sea of life which is the zero point field. To understand the zero point field, you have to get rid of the idea of separateness. You have to rethink your life as a sort of a part of a bigger whole. And you have to understand that your intentions are going to affect your world. Your thoughts affect everything that's going on in your live. So you have to think wisely. We're intrinsic to the whole process of reality. Our involvement creates that reality. We are our world. There is no out there. We are all connected.'

Now to quote **Deepak Chopra**, M.D[7]. and Menas C. Kafatos, Ph.D.[8], co-authors of the book *You Are the Universe: Discovering Your Cosmic Self and Why it Matters.*

Mystery 7: *Do we live in a conscious universe?*

Deepak: *Yes. But this won't make any sense if your notion of a conscious universe is filled with thoughts, sensations, images, and feelings. Those are the contents of the mind. Remove the contents and what remains is pure consciousness, which is silent, unmoving, beyond time and space, yet filled with creative potential. Pure consciousness gives rise to everything, including the human mind. In that sense,* **we don't live in a conscious universe the way renters occupy a rental property. We participate in the same consciousness that is the universe.**

---

[7] Indian medical doctor and writer of books about spirituality and topics in mind-body medicine. Chopra says that he has been influenced by the teachings of Vedanta and the Bhagavad Gita, as well as by Krishnamurti Jiddu, and by the field of quantum physics
[8] Fletcher Jones Endowed Professor of Computational Physics at Champman University and the author of more than 320 refereed articles and fifteen books

CHAPTER 3

THE INTELLIGENCE OF THE HEART

*The mind can only think about wholeness,
but the heart can experience wholeness.*

– Unknown –

*The longest journey you make in your life is
from your head to your heart.*

– Unknown –

Ancient Wisdom and Modern Science About the Heart

(The wisdom of the heart from different perspectives)

> 'The emergence of heart intelligence in society
> will represent a breakthrough in consciousness and understanding,
> leading humanity into a new frontier of perceptual experience and
> transformation.'
>
> – HeartMath institute – Rewriting the Future –

The heart is a supremely important organ. Life starts with the beating of the heart and stops when the heart stops beating. Even if the brain doesn't function, and the heart keeps beating, the person is still alive.

The heart plays a central role in many ways. Look at its role in songs, poems and proverbs. For example:
- Home is where the heart is
- Follow your heart, because it knows your purpose
- Wherever your heart is, there you will find your treasure
- Your heart is your connection with life
- The heart that loves is always young
- The power of your heart is who you are from your deepest essential
- Divine intelligence is in your heart.

The heart is also linked to feelings such as:
- Someone has a broken heart
- Someone died of a broken heart
- It felt like my heart was being torn apart
- Someone has a joyful heart
- Someone is a heartfelt person
- To love someone from the depths of your heart
- To give someone a place in your heart
- Someone's heart is on fire
- Someone touched your heart
- To forgive someone from the depth of your heart
- Your heart is where you find true happiness.

Many books are written about the heart and there are many scientific and imperialist proofs about why the heart is so important. I will review some of them.

The Lotus Sutra or Heart Sutra

In our inner realm of life lies the capacity for important shifts from evil to good, or from good to evil.
This present life,
in which we are born as human beings,
offers us a golden opportunity to ensure
that our lives no longer move along the evil paths,
but instead cross the paths of good.

– Nichiren Daishonin –

In the Lotus Sutra or the Heart Sutra of 2,600 years ago, Shakyamuni Buddha taught his awareness about the heart. According to his teachings, the heart is our treasure tower gifted with the capacity for enlightenment and absolute happiness; feeling happiness in your heart in spite of the circumstances in your life or environment. The human heart is sensitive, versatile and rich, possessing capacities to deliver incredible performance.

Nichiren Daishonin (1222-1282) writes, *But that is precisely why it often undergoes great suffering and torments. In this way the human heart can become entangled in an endless, descending spiral of inner darkness. Does our life continue on the paths of evil forever, or can we succeed in putting it in the path of good? The only way people can change is by overcoming their inner darkness and rediscovering the eternal inviolability and dignity of their own lives. The development of the noble nature with which all people* are originally endowed will immediately lead to a change in the destiny of humanity.

We cannot achieve enlightenment or absolute happiness without making a profound change in our lives. That is, a change in our heart and in our thoughts. The mystical truth to which all living beings are endowed, *the principle of the confinement of a single moment of existence and all phenomena* reveals.

This means that both our lives and our minds embody all phenomena, and they permeate all phenomena at any given moment. One could describe this as a state of life of oneness with the Universe.

Scientific Evidence About the Heart

The Miracle of Life

In *The Miracle of Life*[9], the world's most famous medical photographer and documentary maker Lennart Nilsson portrays the emergence of a new life with unique photo and film material. The recordings were made by means of so-called endoscopic cameras in the body of a pregnant woman. It takes countless steps before a few cells develop into a fully formed child. Nilsson knows how to turn this normally invisible process into a colourful and fantastic spectacle, in which the wonder and complexity of nature are central. *The Miracle of Life* sheds new light on the human instinct of reproduction, fertilization of the egg and the development of the foetus during pregnancy. The unique images make *The Miracle of Life* a classic for a new generation, as it shows how the first organs begin.

---

[9] Studio: WGBH Boston PBS, ASIN: 6302895189, available at https://www.amazon.com/Nova-Miracle-Life-Lennart-Nilsson/dp/6302895189

First comes the heart, together with the liver. Then follows the brain, and next the circulatory system, following which the heart begins to beat before the rest of the body and organs develop.

Initially, all embryos of animals and human beings look the same. From the moment the stem cells transform, you can distinguish the difference in species.

After twenty weeks, the foetus can hear the environment and music. The brains are constantly active. The foetus is dreaming and aware of the environment.

Evidence by HeartMath

> *'As more of humanity practices heart-based living*
> *it will qualify the 'rite of passage'*
> *into the next level of consciousness.*
> *Using our heart's intuitive guidance,*
> *will become common sense*
> *based on practical intelligence.'*
>
> – Doc Childre, Founder of HeartMath Institute –

In 1991, Doc Childre founded the non-profit HeartMath Institute (HMI), a research and education organization. HMI's organizational, educational and clinical research on emotional physiology and self-regulation has been published in peer-reviewed scientific journals and presented at many scientific conferences worldwide.

Recent discoveries have found the heart possesses its own intrinsic nervous system of sensory neurons that can feel, learn and remember, referred to as the *'heart-brain'.* This intelligence processes information independently from the *'head-brain'.* Research at the HMI demonstrated that our intuitive sensitivities are closely tied to this *heart- brain* and our heart's rhythms. A specific rhythmic pattern of the heart, referred to as *'heart coherence'*, has been shown to increase intuitive discernment and improve decision-making skills.

Research has shown that when we're feeling stress, frustration, anger and anxiety, the heart rhythm pattern triggers the brain in a negative way. The measurements show incoherence of the brain function. When we're feeling love, genuine care, compassion, kindness, appreciation, all the qualities we associate with the heart, we see a coherent pattern of the brain function.

Several research projects on intuition replicated by institutions have suggested that heart intuitive processes access a field of information that is not limited by the boundaries of time and space, through the energetic or spiritual heart. It's a source of our deeper intuitive guidance. If we increase our personal coherence, we increase our social coherence and as a result increase global coherence.

The heart has a nerve system, produces hormones, and has a great electromagnetic field which communicates with the brain. During several studies, participants were randomly looking at pictures appearing on the computer. Some were attractive and some were frightening. The 'heart-coherence' reaction came a few seconds *before* they saw the pictures. Which suggests the heart gets information before we can perceive it with our senses.

Prominent medical experts have recently discovered that many recipients of heart transplants are inheriting donors' memories and consequently report huge changes in their tastes, their personality, and, most extraordinarily, in their emotional memories.

For example, a classical violinist was hit by a car and after he received a donor heart, his interest in classical music had gone and he played different music. By asking the family of the donor about his musical preferences, he discovered that he now had the same musical interest as his donor.

Is there another source of intelligence? One that exists outside of us? A field of information which the heart of the person is connected to? I hope someday the scientists will prove it.

PERSONAL LEADERSHIP

CHAPTER 4

THE NINE LAYERS OF CONSCIOUSNESS OF THE LOTUS SUTRA

*The most important problems cannot be solved
within the same framework
in which they were created.*

– Albert Einstein –

The Principle of the Nine Layers[10] of Consciousness
(T'ien T'ai (538-597) nine consciousness concept)

This principle of the nine consciousnesses starts by looking at the way our bodies respond to the world around us, and then considers mental and spiritual processes which explain our behaviour. Fundamentally, however, it tells us that our lives are essentially good, wholesome and pure.

---

[10] *For example, when we are stuck in layer six of mental consciousness and worry about things that happened in the past, wanting to change the past which of course is not possible. Or when we are worrying about the future and see only obstacles that prevent us making decisions in the future or taking steps in the future, we get stuck. What happens is that after a while we get health problems like pain on the shoulders, neck or back. Or we get other emotional problems. When the doctor cannot find the cause of these problems, you can use these layers to find out why you are stuck and visit a professional who can help you to find the source and help you transform it into your power, revealing your hidden potential to take steps to the future.*

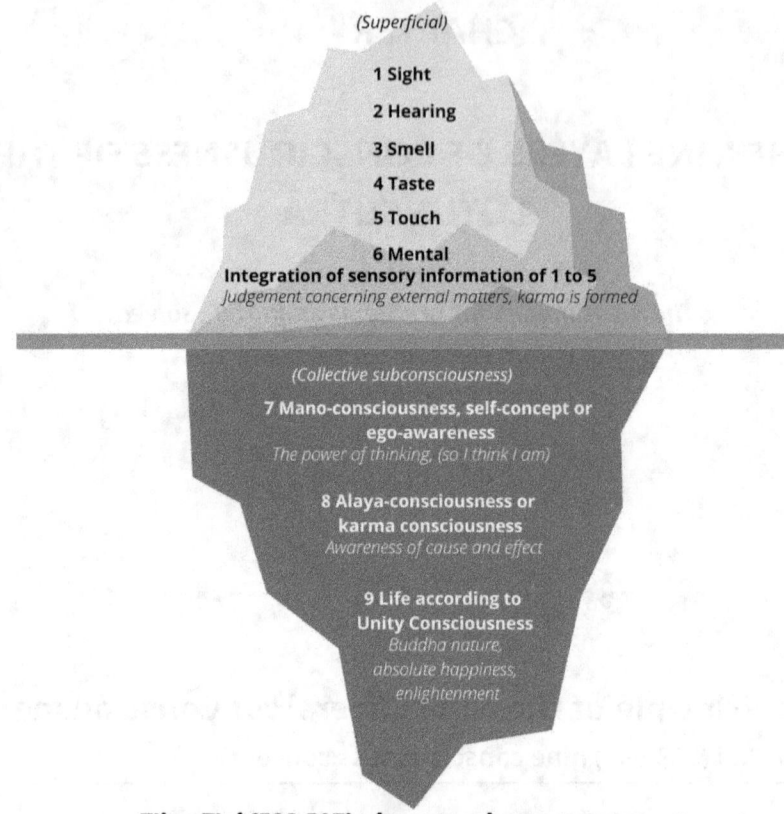

T'ien T'ai (538-597) nine consciousness concept

Introduction

All nine layers of this concept are influencing each other continually. From layer nine to one, there is a hierarchy of energy from forceful to less forceful. The more you can connect with the ninth layer, the more the energy of the other layers will increase to attain greater health, happiness and peace.

Oswald

Oswald, a 47-year old man came to me because his wife couldn't live with his constant complaints about pain in his neck, shoulders and back. For years he went weekly to a physiotherapist to help him release his pain. It only helped for a few hours and then the pain came back on the same level as before. Oswald projected his pain onto his wife, was grumpy all the time and smoked all day long. His wife was allergic to smoke. The pain and cigarettes stood between Oswald and his wife for many years before he came to me.

When he came to me, he explained he had been having therapy for many years already and wondered what I would do differently. I told him that I would not touch or massage him. Rather, I would help him find the source of his pain in his system, in the nine layers. He didn't believe that my approach would help him release the pain he had been carrying since he was fourteen. I told him that it didn't matter if he believed me or not, but it could only work for him if he was open to taking a journey with me to find the source of his pain. He had no choice and agreed.

When I asked him about his family system, he asked me what his family had to do with his pain. At that time, I knew how systems influence people but could not explain. He trusted me and chose to trust my guidance and perspective.

The first session focused on the eighth layer, which is the layer of the family dynamics, and the pain was gone. He came to realise that he had a pattern of carrying all the burdens of his family and other people on his shoulders. He did it unconsciously hence why he was not aware of this pattern in his life. At the age of fourteen his parents were divorced. Oswald was the oldest and lived with his brother and sisters at his mother's house. They were not allowed to visit their father and heard only bad things about him, which Oswald started to believe. He decided to take over the empty space and responsibilities of his father. This pattern was not only in Oswald's own life, but also in past generations. It was the pattern of the oldest child taking over the empty space and responsibilities of a parent who is not able to carry the responsibility himself.

After a few weeks, Oswald returned and told me that he still felt pain but it was less than on the first visit. Because of the insights he got from the sessions with me, he also knew where the pain came from. He told me that he, at the age of forty-seven, was still taking responsibility for his parents on a financial level. They spent more than they could afford and both were in debt. When they got into trouble, they called on Oswald to solve their problems. Oswald was afraid of inheriting the debts of his parents upon their deaths. So, he helped them out.

We worked on the sixth layer of the karma in his own life, because he was a part of the creation of this dynamic. So together, we made a plan. He had a serious conversation with his parents and set up restrictions to protect himself and his future, and handed the responsibly back to his parents, where it belonged. Everything from the past was forgiven. And his pain was gone. Since then, Oswald became aware of the times when people including his parents were putting their burdens onto his shoulders, because the pain returned, but at a lighter level. The pain thus became his compass. He no longer needed my guidance, and his relationship with his wife was full of love again.

Although Oswald was alienated from his father, after his work with me, for the first time, he and his dad could connect on a heart level, the ninth layer. There was unconditional love between them. After six months, his father passed away.

A year later Oswald came to thank me for what he had achieved with my guidance. He told me about his father's funeral and the joy and peace he felt in his heart towards him. They became very close without any animosity between them. It would have been a different funeral if he had not opened himself up to my guidance.

He also came to tell me something I already felt and knew, that he was terminally ill and had only a few months to live. Despite his illness and not being able to solve everything in this lifetime, such as the toxic relationship with his mother, he felt absolute happiness. He had reached the ninth layer.

Thank you, Oswald, for appearing in my life, and for giving me the opportunity to be your guide. I have also learned a lot from you.

Explanation of the Nine Layers of Consciousness

1-5. Layer one to five, Sensory Consciousness

The first five layers represent our five senses: seeing, hearing, smelling, tasting and feeling. These **senses** are vital for **making connection with our inner- and outer worlds**. Both worlds are mirrors of each other. From the perspective of Unity Conscious Leadership™, our outer world is a representation or manifestation of our inner world. I know it's difficult to comprehend. I will explain it later with several examples from my practice.

We use layers one to five to get information from our environment and also to bring back memories and experience them with our senses even though these things happened in the past. This is especially full of memories of significant events in our lives such as births, marriages, funerals, traumas, and other life changing events.

Our senses are the building blocks of our memories. They help in making and recalling memories. For instance: when you smell apple pie, it perhaps reminds you of your grandma, or when you hear a particular song it may remind you of your first love. The emotions of the past unconsciously arise in the here and now.

When I was a young girl, I was bitten by my neighbours' dog. Since then, I no longer trust dogs, especially big ones. In my mind, big dogs were not to be trusted. I became afraid of them and went out of my way to avoid them as they made me nervous. That is how triggers start. After a while we forget what triggered us the first time. The reaction unconsciously comes from our subconscious mind. It works as an automatic pilot, even when we don't think about it. By discovering and solving the trauma, the physical and emotional reaction will disappear.

On a personal level, people can also have opinions about someone they don't know because the person looks like someone they knew in the past. Some people can also feel the energy when they enter a room or have unconscious memories that can make them feel either comfortable or uncomfortable. They are highly sensitive, with senses wide open. Experience with these clients made me aware that there are different drivers to being overly sensitive. Some are born with the gift, some have had a traumatic experience in the past and are almost always in a state of alertness, while others have a combination of both states.

I also have clients who have few or no memories of their youth. Even pictures don't help them memorise their younger years. Mostly it happens after a trauma at a very young age. For them, their youth feels like a gap or a blank page in their timeline. When people are disconnected with their feelings, the information they receive is not entirely complete to integrate into the conscious mind. They integrate what they perceive from four or fewer senses instead of five senses. That is why their memories are distorted because their feelings were not involved to store the experience at that time.

6. Layer six, Mental Consciousness

This layer is also called our conscious mind. Here we integrate our sensory information of layer one to five and make judgements concerning external matters. This is where **karma in this life is formed**. Karma is another word for cause and effect, the seeds of causes we planted in the past which affect us in the future. It's the storeroom where we can store our memories and also recall them through our five senses.

In his book *'Emotional Intelligence'*, Daniel Goleman explains how our brains perceive information from our five senses and transform it into energy that goes to certain parts of our brains, giving emotional meaning to what we perceive at that moment.

The Amygdala is the emotional centre of the brain which triggers fight, flight or freeze when there is an experience of anxiety at any given moment. The Hippocampus is the memory storeroom and the Locus Coeruleus starts making hormones which influences our parasympathetic system, components of which are our heartbeat, breath and blood pressure.

For instance watching an event can bring back memories. *I remember when my daughter had her farewell party at her primary school. She and her schoolmates were dancing and singing on the stage and I was sitting in the audience with all the parents. I was clapping and crying. I felt so* **sad**. *Then I looked to my left and right. I saw everyone else laughing. In the larger area everyone was laughing and seemed to be joyful. I was the only one crying. It was a strange sensation for me. I know now that I was thinking back to how I felt when my son had his farewell party at primary school three years before. I had also cried then. I discovered a pattern in myself about crying and feeling sad at farewell parties at school. Thinking back to my own farewell party at school, I realized I had never had one. I had never said goodbye to my schoolmates in Surinam. We moved to the Netherlands before I could finish primary school in Surinam. Discovering the sadness in myself was the turning point for me from sadness to joy, from crying to smiling.*

John

I was on the participation council of a school together with a few parents. One of the parents expressed concerns about his school to me. He told me that his son John was wobbling restlessly in his chair at school, bobbing up and down, to the annoyance of his teacher.

John was not as bright as the other kids in the class and had to do his best to concentrate and sit quietly. Because his behaviour became so disruptive, the teacher had decided to put him in the hallway as punishment. As a result, he missed lessons and this only made his situation worse.

John was given extra homework and it was always the same repetitive assignments. According to his father, John would sit quietly on his chair at home and finish the assignments. Working through the same assignment was needless repetition from the teacher, because the boy understood everything very well.

John also isolated himself when all his classmates were playing and running around on the schoolyard. He remained standing or sitting in one place. He wasn't happy at school whereas at home, he was happy and played with his brother, sister and friends.

In the meantime, the teacher had urged John's parents at school to have their son tested psychologically. According to this teacher, his cognitive capacity was less developed than that of his peers and perhaps he also had a behavioural disorder. Depending on the outcome of the tests, the school was able to acquire resources (a 'backpack' or financial contribution from the government) to be able to guide him in a more targeted way, once the teacher knew in which 'disorder box' to place him. His parents did not agree but the teacher told them that these were the rules at school.

I listened to the story and asked him if John had ever visited an optician to have his sight tested. I sensed it could be a vision problem.

A week or so later I saw John happily playing and running around with his friends on the schoolyard. He had glasses on his nose. John could finally sit quietly in the classroom, able to concentrate well and developed faster than his peers.

As a member of the representative advisory board, I introduced this case to the meeting with the request to perform visual and auditory tests in addition to psychological tests, because these tests stop at a consultation centre after a certain age. The school said that it was the parents' responsibility and were even reluctant to inform parents about these possibilities.

How many children would get rid of a 'label' as a result? And how many children would flourish and increase their potential as a result? Unfortunately, I will never know. I am glad I was able to make a difference in John's case though.

7. Layer seven, Mano-consciousness or self-concept

This is also called ego-awareness or subconsciousness. It is where the power of thought resides. The seventh layer is about interpretation, how you give meaning to a manifestation.

Maria

Maria was nearly fifty years old. At her father's funeral, she was aware the people were crying over the loss of her father, yet though she felt sad, she was unable to cry. She realized she had never cried in her life. Sadness was an emotion she could not express. It was blocked. She also discovered that she projected her sadness onto her husband by getting angry with him for no reason. Maria knew her husband was innocent and wanted to break through this destructive pattern. This was why she came to see me at my practice.

During a session she realized she had not been allowed to cry since she was a baby. Her biological mother kept her secret and nobody was allowed to know about her existence. Her mother taped her mouth with adhesive tape whenever she started crying. Eventually, a foreign couple discovered Maria and adopted her when she was a few months old and raised her.

At the end of the session Maria's first teardrops started to flow. She felt released, a sense of peace came over her and she could literally see everything more clearly. Since then, Maria has been able to cry when she is sad. Her projection of anger towards her husband, whom she loves very much, has disappeared.

8. Layer eight, Alaya – or karma consciousness

Also called the Ground Consciousness, where afflictive behaviours and interpretations can be reinforced. The story of Oswald at the beginning of this chapter is an example of patterns on the eighth layer. Breaking through the patterns on the eighth layer transforms the patterns on all layers.

Daisaku Ikeda on the Eighth layer of Consciousness;

Both good karma and bad karma are stored there like seeds in a granary. The term 'storehouse' conjures the image of an actual structure into which things of substance can be placed. But in fact, it may be more accurate to say that the life-current of karmic energy itself constitutes the eighth consciousness. (Daisaku Ikeda in: Wisdom of The Lotus Sutra, p.35)

My own experiences and also those of my clients have shown that the karmic energy of cause and effect stored in the eighth layer is a storehouse of collective memories of past generations. It's **the repository of the effects of causes created in our eternal past.** Here is the **starting point of perpetuating patterns in our lives in the here and now.** It's where we find the source of darkness and delusion arising from our desires. That is why it's important to be aware of desires. Here lies the 'hidden treasure' which reveals itself when the darkness and delusion is solved.

Only love and fear exists here. When people are stuck in their thinking, they are detached from their hearts. If they choose love, they go to their Buddha nature or absolute happiness, the ninth layer.

9. Layer nine, Absolute Happiness

This layer is also called Buddha nature, enlightenment, unchangeable reality, the fundamental, original and absolutely pure consciousness which is universal and constitutes the essence of our lives, love, joy, increased vitality, courage, wisdom and compassion. A bundle of energy with the greatest potential at our core.

Without tapping the ninth layer, our destiny lies in the eighth – and is fixed.

Relative and Absolute Happiness

There is really only one kind of happiness,
that is absolute happiness.

– Joyce Z. Wazirali –

Relative Happiness

Once I was on my way back home from holiday. I asked the man sitting next to me how he felt about his holiday. He said he went on holiday to 'charge his battery'. The first few days of his holiday, he wound down from the pressure of his working life. Once he relaxed, he felt good and happy. But the thoughts about going back to work soon unsettled him and made him restless again.

I know people who buy clothes to make themselves feel happy again. Others buy a new car or a bigger house, find a new love, eat food, smoke a cigarette, drink a glass of wine, sport intensively to feel happiness. After a while, the feeling of happiness disappears and the stress returns.

These are all examples of relative happiness.

I quote Daisaku Ikeda; *'Relative happiness is fleeting and transient. No matter how rich a person is, a drastic social change can make someone gain fear overnight. An apparently healthy person can have an accident or suddenly get sick. And as we get older, we often have to deal with some kind of illness.*

Relative happiness is based on our circumstances. If our circumstances change, we can easily lose this happiness. Even though we imagine we have everything we want, whilst we cannot control our desires, when we achieve something, our happiness will be short-lived, and we will find ourselves 'wanting' again. Strong attachment to wealth and matter can make a person spiritually poor. Relative happiness only exists in relation to external factors. That is why it is called 'relative happiness'.

Absolute Happiness

I remember my mother-in-law (and best friend) sitting next to me on the couch during her last earthly days. She looked at me and said:; *Joyce, I am in a lot of pain and there is so much misery around me. Yet, for some reason despite the circumstances I feel so happy. I have never felt this way. My heart is overflowing with love.* Her eyes were sparkling, her face was relaxed, and there was a big smile on her face.

I told her: Yes, I can see it. Although you suffer from pain, you look absolutely beautiful and much younger. I knew that she was ready to leave earthly life.

Sitting next to her, I saw and felt absolute happiness.

I quote Daisaku Ikeda again: *'Absolute happiness is indestructible, does not depend on our constantly changing circumstances. It is unchangeable, a sense of fulfilment and satisfaction at the deepest level of our existence. That we can experience, regardless of our circumstances, that life itself is joy. When we reach this state of life, our lives will sparkle with joy, vitality, courage, wisdom and compassion. Even though we may have great difficulties or struggle with an illness, none of those circumstances will discourage us and we will experience a state of joy, fulfilment and satisfaction. That is absolute happiness. If you have a strong life force and wisdom it is possible to overcome challenges and trials in the same way that high waves make surf exciting and steep rocks make mountain climbing exhilarating.'*

General

Layer one to nine can be likened to an iceberg; with layer one to six at the surface and the other layers beneath the surface.

Layers seven to nine are the layers of the collective subconsciousness. Without us being aware of it, the collective subconsciousness influences our lives, our behaviour and who we are in the here and now.

A change in layer one to five can make a change in layer six.

A change in the sixth layer will change the first five layers and may affect the seventh layer.

A change in the seventh layer will change the first six layers and may affect the eighth layer.

A transformation in the eight layer will transform all the other layers and bring you more into the ninth layer.

Layer six to nine are unconscious layers. We are not aware of them unless we investigate them by self-reflection from the perspective of Unity Conscious Leadership™.

CHAPTER 5

UNITY CONSCIOUS LEADERSHIP™ CONCEPT OF SUFFERING AND TRANSFORMATION

The greatest danger in time of turbulence
is not the turbulence,
it is to act with yesterday's logic.
– Peter Drucker –

Concept of Personal Suffering and Transformation
(According to my own experiences, insights, dreams and visions)

Unity Conscious Leadership

(Layers of suffering)

1 Mental
Mostly in the head, thinking a lot

2 Social
Experiencing difficulties in relationships

3 Emotional
Feeling of stress and danger

4 Physical
Unexplainable pain

5 Spiritual
Based on Dualism, separation of self and environment

(Layer of transformation)
6 Unity Conscious Leadership™
The solution lies in the problem

working on:
a new and higher awareness,
awareness of cause and effect,
breaking through obstructing patterns in life
on soul level,
transcending duality,
revealing our greatest potential at
our core,
finding love, joy, increased
vitality, courage, wisdom
and compassion,
absolute happiness,
enlightenment

Concept of the layers of personal suffering and transformation (of *Joyce Z. Wazirali*)

Explanation of the Layers of Suffering and Tansfomation

*When your inner resolve changes,
everything is transformed.*

– Wolfgang von Goethe –

Unity Conscious Leadership™ Concept of Suffering and Transformation

Introduction

I will explain the five layers of suffering and one layer of transformation with practical examples from my work with my clients.

First of all, my clients had been to the doctor and had therapy elsewhere. Despite their effort to break through their obstructing patterns and the pain and suffering in their lives, there was no change. They had heard about me and were wondering how I could help them. For every client I was able to offer a tailor-made solution therapy, which they found helpful.

It took years for me to explain how I do what I do and why it is successful. Even at this moment, while I am writing this book, I am still puzzling to find answers to my own question, 'how best to explain'?

What I discovered

What I discovered in my many years' experience is that there is always a trauma behind the layers of suffering. Traumas that want to be resolved. Within the trauma, potential is locked, something most people are longing for but cannot reach for some reason. Lost potential that they need, to take steps towards their future and give them direction in their lives. When the trauma is healed and the potential gets unlocked, people thrive, become resilient, adaptable to change and more able to reach their goals.

Layers of Suffering

1. Mental suffering

People who are suffering mentally are mostly in their heads, thinking all the time. They are worrying about certain things in life, lacking focus and losing contact with their bodies. Walking through life as though they are in another world, missing the connection with their environment.

They worry about different things, such as events in the past, the present or the future. They listen to their repeating inner voices with obstructing beliefs, judging other people and situations. Trying to change their environment. They often experience headaches.

Hilda

Hilda was sixty years old when she came to my practice with the question why she was almost always rejected by her loved ones and her environment. It had been a common thread in her life since she was a child. Every time it happened, she felt left out, abandonment, lonely and had a sense of emptiness in herself. She was desperate to belong to and be loved by her loved ones. Her feeling of loneliness and sadness grew more and more every day. Not knowing how to stop this train of thought, she had been locked up all her life.

She created her own strategy to connect with her environment. Before she approached anyone, she started thinking what to say, when to say it, and how to say it. At the same time, she had already prepared herself for the rejection that influenced her tone, words and behaviour. It made her appear dominant. Which was not her intention.

Hoping to be liked, she tried even harder to help others even if they didn't ask. She was stuck in a vicious circle which she couldn't get out of and it got worse and worse. She was thinking all the time which made her very tired.

From the point of view of Unity Conscious Leadership™, I suggested that something in *her* needed to change instead of her environment. Deep down, she already knew this, but she didn't know how to change.

She was born in France as the oldest of six children. At a young age her parents were divorced. Her father left his children behind and never showed up again. Her mother became a single mother with six young children and had to take care of them. This meant she wasn't able to work and as a single mother at that time, she couldn't get financial support from the government. The only thing she could do was to take her children to a childcare house and leave them there.

After two years, Hilda was adopted by a couple in a foreign country. Her adoptive parents also spoke French, but everyone else in her environment spoke a different language. It was difficult for her to make friends. Although her adoptive mother loved her very much, she felt lonely and sad. During her whole life she encountered situations where the feeling of loneliness and sadness came up.

We worked on her traumas to break through the obstructing patterns in her life, which were the sources of her feeling of loneliness and sadness. Later she heard from someone who knew her parents, that this pattern was not only hers, but also of her biological parents of whom she had no memory.

After the therapy, the feelings of loneliness, sadness and emptiness were gone. She was filled with self-love. Since then, when someone says 'no' to her, she no longer feels abandoned. She doesn't always need people around her, can be alone, enjoys life more, is happy and laughs more often. She accepts when someone doesn't have time for her. She's relaxed and not doing her utmost to make people like her. And finally, she doesn't worry anymore.

2. Social suffering

People who experience social suffering have difficulties making contact with their environment. They don't know how to connect or haven't learned to connect since childhood. When they try to connect, they feel uncomfortable and get stressed.

Peter

Seven years ago at the age of seventy-two, Peter came to me. Several people recommended me to him. The first time he came, he was very nervous but he could not back out. He knew he had made a mess of his own life, the lives of his ex-wives and those of his adult children. He had gathered the courage to tell me everything he had done wrong.

He started with, *I want to connect with my children, but I don't know how. I am an alcoholic, have not fulfilled my promises in the past and didn't take responsibility as a father and husband. Because of what I did or did not do, I feel very lonely. I don't know what love is. How could I give love to my wife and children if I have never felt love? My wish is to make a journey to my heart. To feel love in my heart so I can connect with myself and my children from my heart.*

This journey took seven years. He came a few times per year to me and bit by bit there was a progression. First, he stopped drinking which was very difficult for him after fifty-six years addiction. He had started to drink when he began to feel the emptiness within himself. When he drank, the emptiness was gone for a while. This empty feeling was a result of missing the love and connection with his own parents. This was a pattern for generations.

We started a program of Unity Conscious Leadership™. First, we worked on breaking through obstructing patterns he inherited from generations before him, which replaced the emptiness he felt with love from his ancestors. As a result, it became easier for him to overcome his withdrawal symptoms of alcohol addiction. Then we worked on several traumas in his younger years. He became more aware of how Unity Conscious Leadership™ works and was thriving.

One day he came to me and told me that his feeling of emptiness had gone. But he didn't feel love for his children yet. He worked on the blockages in his own system towards his children and also his environment. There were also sessions of forgiveness. These were all one-to-one sessions. The next step for him was to confess what he discovered he didn't do right towards his children. So, he organized a gathering with his children and grandchildren. Without going into details, he told them how sorry he was, and that he had undergone therapy to break through his old bad habits. He explained that he forgave himself and hoped his children could forgive him also.

A few weeks after the gathering he came to my practice to tell me how it went and thanked me for the guidance to his heart. He finally could feel the love for his children and grandchildren. I could see him radiate unconditional love. "By the way" he said: "If I should die tomorrow, I will never regret I've made this journey to my heart". He thanked me. After a month, he was diagnosed with cancer.

For reasons of his own, he was not ready to go yet. He went to the mother of his children and confessed everything to her and hoped she would forgive him.

The feeling of absolute love was always there, and he used the last months of his life to give his children and grandchildren something he could not give before. Six months later, at the age of seventy-nine he left earthly life without fear and with a great sense of happiness.

Peter's funeral was peaceful and there was a lot of respect for what he had done to not only help himself, but also to help his descendants to live a happier and more peaceful life.

Thank you, Peter, for your courage and trust.

3. Emotional suffering

People who are emotionally suffering feel continuous stress and are very alert. They live keeping a close eye on their environment, because they don't feel safe and are always in fight, flight or freeze mode.

Danny

Danny from Belgium was eighteen years when he came to my practice. He had mostly aggressive people around him, and for no apparent reason, he was beaten by other boys. He was slim and tall and didn't look as though he wanted to fight with anyone. Danny was very stressed and sad. Deep inside him was a feeling of anger that ignited rapidly.

Having a conversation with him was a challenge. Because he spoke very softly, with his jaws clamped. I had to drag the answers to my questions from him.

At school he had problems with concentration, was unaware of his talents and lacked motivation and direction for his future. He was always busy trying to survive while he was longing to feel free, enjoy life and find direction. But something was holding him back.

When we met, I told him how Unity Conscious Leadership™ works and if he wanted to get free from his obstructive environment, he had to find the source of this manifestation in himself. Although he had never looked at his problems that way, he trusted me and surrendered himself to my guidance.

The pattern we discovered started with his great grandmother who lived in Angola. She was a successful businesswoman. She thrived and her business flourished. However, because of a war, she and her family lost everything, including love ones who were killed in the war. This caused sadness, fear, anger and poverty.

Danny had the same patterns and feelings that his great-grandmother had experienced after the war. Although he was raised in another country and in peace, he didn't feel safe. We worked on the family trauma, breaking through patterns which were passed through the generations. Eventually the tension and anger were gone and he began to feel more relaxed.

Danny feels safe now, is doing very well, and is happy and cheerful. He no longer gets angry and doesn't walk away from difficult situations. When he doesn't grasp a situation or understand a person, he starts asking questions. He talks more loudly and is understandable. The direction for his future has become clear for him.

Thank you, Danny, for who you are.

4. Physical suffering

There are people who suffer physically without an explanation about where it comes from. Despite massage, the physical pain keeps coming back. From experience I know that people who are cut from their emotions will only realize when it gets worse and the body starts to ache.

Richard

Richard was in his fifties. A father of three children around twenty. When his kids were small, he liked to cuddle and touch them a lot. His kids liked that, and they had a lot of joy together.

One day, however, he stopped cuddling and touching them. A fear came over him he could not place and did not understand. The kids missed physical contact with their father and the relationship changed as a result.

Richard wanted to find out why he acted the way he did. During the session he realized he was abused by someone when he was at the same age as his children were when he stopped cuddling them.

He worked on his trauma. After that he was able to make physical contact with his children and could cuddle them again.

Because Richard became open to connecting with his children again, the relationship between them improved.

Christiana

At the age of thirty-five, Christiana came to my practice. She suffered from pains on several levels. Christiana had been short of breath for as long as she could remember, lots of thoughts came to her mind, she could not stay focused, couldn't feel her inner power and was always looking for someone to lean on. She had also several depressions and a feeling of emptiness inside.

During our sessions she realized she had missed her father since she was a little girl. Her father was often at work and when he was at home, he didn't pay attention to her. Christiana missed the connection with her father because she didn't receive love and support from him. Just as her father missed the connection and love from his father, her grandfather, at a young age.

Her grandfather had to leave the country because of poverty. As a small child, Christiana's father moved with his parents (her grandparents) to another country. It was an abrupt and traumatic move for him. He had to leave not only the place he was raised, but also his friends and safe environment.

Every time Christiana's father looked at her, she reminded him of the trauma and pain of missing his father, losing his dear friends and safe environment as a child. It happened unconsciously but nevertheless influenced his behaviour towards Christiana. To avoid his own pain, her father kept his focus on everything except her.

After working with me, Christiana could breathe deeply for the first time in her life, felt powerful, relaxed and focused. The feeling of emptiness was gone, and she was filled with a feeling she had never felt before. She felt love, self-love! And the relationship with her father changed in a positive way.

Loraine

Loraine was fifteen years old and at secondary school. One day her mother called me to ask for help for Loraine. She told me that Loraine suffered from pain at the right side of her belly. Exactly where the pain is felt with appendicitis. I asked her a few questions and my conclusion was that Loraine had appendicitis. Then her mother told me that Loraine had already been in hospital for a week, and that the doctors had examined her but could not find a medical cause for the pain. It was definitely not appendicitis, so they would not operate on her. Because the pain was very severe and the doctors had no idea how to help, Loraine was allowed to leave the hospital for a week and lie in her own bed at home.

Instead of driving home with Loraine, her mother chose to drive her to my practice. She thought, if the cause was not physical, then it must be on another level. When she arrived at my practice, Loraine could not walk upright because she was in so much pain. After I asked her a few questions and connected with her on an energetic level, I realized she had problems in relationships. So, I asked her if she currently had problems with relationships. That was when she revealed her biggest secret, one she had kept from her mother for months. She was being bullied at school by a group of girls. She was so anxious that she would rather disappear. She had already missed school for a few weeks, the results of her tests were poor, and she ended up in a downward spiral. For the first time she was open to her mother about what had happened at school.

At the end of the first session her pain decreased considerably. She could stand and walk more upright.

We did more sessions, and she was reconnected with her inner force. She felt strong and vivid again. Together with the principal of the school she had a conversation with the girls who bullied her. Her pain was gone, and she caught up with her schoolwork. The girls never bullied her again.

After one week she went back to the hospital for a check. The doctors could not find an explanation why the pain suddenly disappeared. Loraine never told the doctors about her sessions with me and how she solved the cause of the pain.

Andy

I had known Andy since he was a little boy. He was in his thirties when he came to me with complaints about pain in his neck and shoulders. He had tried to get rid of the pain using different kinds of physical therapy. But nothing worked. The pain worsened. He couldn't even turn his head at this point. It was like his neck and shoulders were fixed and the pain cost him so much energy that he could not do his job properly. He asked me to help because he didn't know what else to do.

Andy also had a deep wish to have a relationship with his first love, Sasha. They split up and Andy always compared his new girlfriends with Sasha. In the past he already had several short relationships with Sasha, but each ended in separation. He wanted to break through this pattern.

During the sessions, Andy recognized that, when he was about four, his father had suffered a car accident and was unable to work because of disability. As the oldest child, Andy promised his father he would take the responsibility for the family. He also promised his mother he would marry her later!

We worked on the burdens of his parents that Andy took on his shoulders and neck. The pain in his shoulders and neck disappeared. He was surprised that without touching or massage, the pain was gone. He could turn his head to the left and right without any pain. His head was relaxed, and he was free of worries.

Andy had also cancelled his promise to his mother to marry her one day. He felt that he could be the child of his parents again. It gave him a feeling of freedom to walk his own life path just as it was meant to be.

A few weeks later, he told me that the pain around his shoulders and neck had not come back. He used the lessons he learned to leave the burdens of others to others and to carry his own burdens. He also used the pain he felt in the past as his compass. Whenever the pain threatened to come back, he asked himself whose burdens he was carrying. By handing them back, the pain was relieved. The greater news was that Andy and Sasha were together again as a couple. And as I write their story twenty years after helping Andy, Andy and Sasha have been happily married for fifteen years and have four lovely children.

5. Spiritual suffering based on Dualism

Sometimes people get hit by situations in their lives they cannot declare. It's like a shift on their pathway. It happens over and over again like a pattern that never ends despite the actions taken in the past. It's invisible and people keep experiencing perpetuating obstructing patterns in life. In their search for common ground and a declaration of the shifts in their lives, they start looking for answers between the conscious and subconscious level. Mostly looking for answers from the perspective of dualism, they see themselves as separated from their environment. They try to break through the pattern by trying to change their environment expecting the people around them to change or just moving to another environment. Sometimes it helps to take a step to a new environment. Mostly the patterns come again and again. For generations.

Eleonora

Eleonora was in the forties when she came to my practice. She had been happily married to her husband for almost twenty years. Her biological clock was ticking, and she and her husband were longing to have a child. But somewhere in the back of her mind, Eleonora was anxious about separation after their baby was born. To end up like a single mother, taking care of her child alone. That had been a pattern in her family line. Thus, she wanted to break through this pattern, before risking having a child.

During the sessions, she realized she was carrying a burden from past generations. Even generations she knew nothing about. It all started with a love affair of her great-great-grandmother who worked as a slave. Her slave owner and she fell in love with each other. Her great-great-grandmother got pregnant by her slave-owner and lover. Because their love affair had to be kept secret, by the time her child was born, she had been abandoned by her lover. Although there was love between them, the slave holder sold her to another slave-owner. So, the pattern of abandonment started with Eleonora's great-great-grandmother and the birth of her great-grandmother.

This story was never told, until six months after the sessions with me. Her mother confirmed this story, which had already been revealed during our sessions.

Eleonora's feeling of anxiety disappeared when she came to understand what had happened and she no longer had to carry the burden of her great-great-grandmother.

Layer of Transformation

6. Unity Conscious Leadership™, the transformational layer

The Solution lies in the problem.
You only have to find the key to the Solution.
The key is Unity Conscious Leadership™.

– Joyce Z. Wazirali –

Ever since I started guiding people and organizations to grow and thrive, I became aware of the story behind their behaviour by watching, listening and sensing the drivers within them. With the conviction that the solution lies in the problem, I found my own way to discover the key to the solutions. More recently, I became aware that is has a name: 'Unity Conscious Leadership™'. Most of the time, my clients succeeded in breaking through their obstructing patterns in their lives and businesses. I've also had clients who used drugs in their younger years with irreversible brain damage. Unfortunately, I couldn't help them entirely.

General

Layer one to four, mental, social, emotional and physical: you can become aware of layer one to four with your senses (through seeing, hearing, and feeling). By the words people use to express themselves, their behaviour and actions. Such as: *I think I am feeling well* (express their physical feelings from a mental state of mind); *I don't like those people, or I don't feel safe with those people around me* (express their relationship on a social level); *thinking about going to work makes me feel stressed* (express their emotions towards a situation); *taking the* *responsibility for the team feels like a burden on my shoulder* (express physical complaints towards a situation).

Layer five spiritualism based on Dualism (separation of self and environment): layer five is invisible but tangible through the experience of perpetuating obstructing patterns in life. Here mostly people are in search of new insights, and answers to build a bridge between the conscious and subconscious level, them and I, person and environment.

Layers one to five of suffering influence each other all the time. For example, if there is mental suffering, it always influences the social-, emotional-, physical- and spiritual layers, and so forth.

Layer six, Unity Conscious Leadership™; is the layer of transformation. Here, the solution is *trapped* in the problem. Layer six is invisible. You can experience it in your life and feel it in your heart by working on *a new and higher awareness, awareness of cause and effect, breaking through perpetuating obstructing patterns in life on soul level, transcending duality, revealing our greatest potential at our core, finding love, joy, increased vitality, courage, wisdom and compassion, growing to absolute happiness and enlightenment.*

Merging Eastern Wisdom with Western Knowledge

Unity Conscious Leadership™ is the linking pin between the nine layers of consciousness concept of T'ien T'ai based on the Lotus Sutra, and the layers of suffering and transformation.

Eastern Wisdom

The source of suffering always lies on layers six to eight of the nine layers of consciousness. For some reason I was already aware of these layers by observing my world through the *lens of* Unity Conscious Leadership™. This perspective helps me to find the root cause of the problems of my clients.

Western Knowledge

The layers of suffering are, from the perspective of Unity Conscious Leadership™, where the suffering is expressed, gets triggered or arises. I have used Western Knowledge and interventions with the lens of Unity Conscious Leadership™, to work with my clients for solutions to their problems.

Transcending dualism for more health, happiness and peace

By merging the Eastern Wisdom and Western knowledge with the lens of Unity Conscious Leadership™, a new opportunity arises to transcend mutual differences for more health, happiness and peace. Unity Conscious Leadership™ is a state of life everyone can decide to step into.

Seven Steps for Personal Unity Conscious Leadership™

1. Mirror
Perceive your outer world as the mirror of your inner world.

2. Find your trigger(s)
Every person or situation that triggers you by taking you out of balance, creating arousal or bringing back negative emotions like anger, pain, suffering, anxiety, etcetera, is a starting point for reflection.

3. Self-Reflection
Start with your own reflection: *what are my thoughts, feelings and actions that are represented by the trigger(s)?* You can use the list of examples of patterns and behaviour on personal level in chapter 1.

4. Introspection
Take the insights of your reflection for introspection. Ask yourself: *when and in which context* (family, friends, working place, and so on) *did I experience this before?* You can use the list of examples of paradoxes and behaviour in organizations in chapter 1.

5. Patterns
Discover the patterns in your life and through the lives of your ancestors.

6. Transform through Unity Conscious Leadership™
Find a qualified professional who understands and practices Unity Conscious Leadership™ and can apply the right intervention for your problem, or contact me on www.unityconsciousleadership.com or www.eenheidbewustleiderschap.nl.

7. Make it generative
Take the insights you get from the transformation and share your experience with others who could benefit from it.

Unity Conscious Leadership™ Concept of Suffering and Transformation

CULTURAL LEADERSHIP

CHAPTER 6

CULTURAL LEADERSHIP FROM A BUDDHIST PERSPECTIVE

The greater the suppression of an aspect,
the more distorted this aspect presents itself.
So every non-lived aspect
comes undisguised, distorted, judgmental, pervasive or secretly.
Only by illuminating this shadow
can this aspect exist in its
true sense.

– Carl Gustav Jung –

My Early Experiences With Cultures

We are not only a part of our culture,
we are the creators of our culture.

– Joyce Z. Wazirali –

My childhood

Ever since my childhood I have learned how to build a flourishing world of great diversity of nature and people and reside in it.

I was born and (until my tenth year) raised in the Amazon in Surinam, a multi-cultural country in South America.

Besides the diversity of nature, I also had the opportunity to grow up in a part of the world with a diversity of people, food, music, art, languages, descendants of different parts of the world, religions, cultures with their own habits, norms, values and beliefs. Surinam is a melting pot of diversity in many ways, with the native Indians and descendants from Africa, India, Indonesia, China, Lebanon, the Netherlands and other countries. The main religions practised are Hinduism, Protestantism, Catholicism and other Christian denominations, Islam, Judaism, Maroon religions, and Indigenous religions.

In Paramaribo, the capital city of Surinam, you will find three churches of different religions built next to each other. A mosque, a synagogue and a cathedral. People respect their religions, learn from other cultures, join each other's feasts and integrate aspects of different cultures into their own lives.

Of course, there has also been violence between people. Mostly because of the desire for power and dominance over others. This has nothing to do with diversity but is due to individualism. It was always a minority, which is why, in the end, the merger of diversity overcame the violence.

The Netherlands

When I was ten, our whole family emigrated to the Netherlands. Surinam was by that time a colony of the Netherlands and everyone spoke Dutch. We came into a country with a different culture, climate and nature. I remember my first New Year's Eve with family in The Hague. I was looking through the windows of the apartment on the fourth floor when I saw a naked man running around. It was freezing. I found it very strange and asked myself, is this normal? The police soon came and captured the man. I realized it was not normal to be running naked through the streets.

For the first time of my life, I saw snow and the changing of the seasons. I learned to be resilient and adaptable to change.

Reflections from my first journey in Surinam

My ancestral roots are in Asia, North and South America (Amazon and Andes native Indians), Alaska and Europe. My visit to Suriname made me realize where I come from and how the basis of my perspective on life was reflected by the indigenous Amazon Indians, my ancestors.

In 2014, after forty years, I returned to Surinam. One of the places I visited was Galibi, where the native Indians still live as we used to see them in the movies. Although they slept in huts, they had Wi-Fi and modern devices such as computers and iPhones. They kept their basic norms and values to teach the children to live in Unity Consciousness. This was the prayer at the primary school. From the age of four, all the children started their school day with:

Good father,

Creator of heaven and earth,
We thank you for the last night's rest
and for this new day.

We ask you for knowledge and insight,
health and strength for everything
that we will do today.

Give us more love so that we
all big and small in your name
be one.
Amen

St Antonius School, Galibi

Connecting the dots with the Lotus Sutra

Have you ever wondered;

- Why are people and organizations falling back into old habits and patterns?
- Why is it so difficult to transcend mutual differences?
- How can we break through obstructive situations in life and business?

These were the questions I have been asking myself ever since I was a child. I discovered that the answers were already in the questions. The only way to find the answers is by changing our perspective on life.

At a young age I started to see patterns and interdependence in nature and between people. Seeing these patterns makes it not only easy for me to find the cause and required solutions to problems, but also makes future events predictable to me. I thought everyone could see that.

Later at school and in my professional life, I was a little bit different from my colleagues. Because of how I perceive situations, my thoughts and answers to questions are different.

Mostly people didn't understand my way of thinking. On the other hand, I thought, it's so obvious what I was perceiving, why couldn't they see that?

It was as if I was looking at the world through a different 'lens'. In retrospect, it turned out to be my gift. I always used this 'lens' unconsciously, until I discovered it while I was writing this book.

It took me more than five decades to give words to my perspective on life. I would love to share my *best kept secret* about the complexity of life and thus the complexity of culture in this chapter with you.

What helped me to give words to Unity Conscious Leadership™ was the practice and deepening understanding of Nichiren Buddhism.

Since my childhood, I have had dreams about Shakyamuni Buddha. I could not place these experiences until I was accidentally introduced to Nichiren Buddhism, which explains the Wisdom of the Lotus Sutra of 2,600 years ago.

The Lotus Sutra explains the complex *coherence of life*, which I have always perceived and been aware of, but was not able to put into words until now.

The Emergence of Culture

The monkeys and the bananas

I am aware of an experiment with monkeys to elaborate on organizational culture. Some say it's a real event or experiment conducted by R.G. Stephenson, while others believe it's a fable. I am not sure which opinion is the correct one. However, I still think it's useful to look at it as a metaphor.

A group of psychologists performed an experiment years ago. They started with a cage containing five monkeys. Inside the cage, they hung a banana on a string with a set of steps placed beneath it. Before long, one of the monkeys went to the steps and started to climb towards the banana. As soon as he did, the psychologists sprayed the other monkeys with ice-cold water. The psychologists used the ice-cold water as punishment, knowing that monkeys don't like to get wet. After a while, another monkey attempted to obtain the banana. As soon as his foot touched the steps, all of the other monkeys were sprayed with ice-cold water. It wasn't long before the other monkeys physically prevented any monkey from climbing the steps.

Now, the psychologists shut off the cold water, removed one monkey from the cage and replaced it with a new one. The new monkey saw the banana and started to climb the steps. To his surprise and horror, the other monkeys attacked him. After another attempt and attack, he clearly realised, that if he tried to climb the steps, he would be assaulted, and he didn't try again. Next, the scientists removed another of the original five monkeys and replaced it with a new one. The same thing happened, and this time, the previous newcomer *also took part in the punishment*. Finally, the scientists replaced a third original monkey with a new one, then a fourth, then the fifth.

Every time the newest monkey tried to climb the steps, he was attacked. Of course, the monkeys had no idea why they were not permitted to climb the steps or why they were attacking any monkey that tried. After replacing all the original monkeys, none of the remaining monkeys had ever been sprayed with cold water. Nevertheless, no monkey ever again approached the steps to try for the banana. Why not? Because as far as they know, *that's the way it's always been around here.*

Unwritten rules cause undercurrent

This is an example of how unwritten rules are created. Rules that we have gained by experience or that someone else had talked about, comprise unwritten norms, values and beliefs everyone in the organization is supposed to follow.

These unwritten rules influence our collective behaviour. Newcomers to a team or organization experience the unwritten rules as an *organizational undercurrent*. After a while they adjust to the situation and think: *this is the way it is here. I have to accept it.*

Influence of Those Who are Responsible

The influence of the group of psychologists on culture and behaviour is remarkably interesting in this experiment. They were in control and created the culture in which the monkeys were caught. They knew what they were doing was to prove something they already expected. The psychologists were also a part of the culture and behaviour, even though they were not visible to the monkeys in the cage.

Let's look at this situation from the perspective of the monkeys. They were prohibited from using their talents in the given environment. If they tried to use them, they were punished. The psychologists did it on purpose of course, it was their hidden agenda. By prohibiting the monkeys from using their talents, the psychologists took away the freedom of the monkeys to be at their best.

Suppose the punitive psychologists are later replaced with positive psychologists encouraging the monkeys to use their talents and be at their best. In the short term, the monkeys would try but would then fall back into their old pattern of anxiety and do nothing. Because what happened previously is already a blueprint of the collective memory of the organization and nothing has been changed on the collective level.

Practical example

I once had a client who took over a company with several departments. He couldn't handle department X and fired the whole team at once. He replaced them with a new group. When he told me what he did, I warned him that his action would not be the solution he wanted but make things worse for the whole company. Within six months, the whole department would be replaced again.

Although people didn't know each other or anything about the previous situation, the same pattern began to emerge in department X. The staff from other departments became anxious that they too would get fired. The best ones quit the company, having found jobs elsewhere, others suffered illness, and/or failed to perform effectively and made more and more mistakes.

After six months my forecast became reality. The director didn't want to look at his own and his predecessors' influence on the situation in the company or take heed of my advice. He did not suffer financially because it was a non-profit organization. So, I stopped advising him.

Who Makes the Culture?

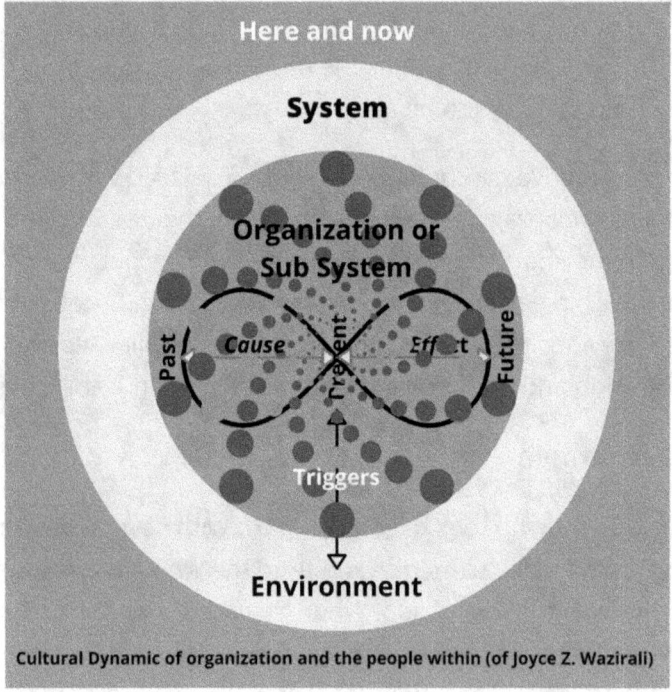

Cultural Dynamic of organization and the people within (of Joyce Z. Wazirali)

An organization (or subsystem of a larger system) is a cooperation between two or more people to achieve a common goal. It can be a sports club, workplace, special activity, friendship, family gatherings, school, the schoolyard, etc.

People in the past *and* present were and are the creators of cultural organizations. Everyone who once was and is part of the organization leaves or puts an invisible blueprint in the collective memory of the organization. Due to the invisible blueprint, perpetuating patterns are created over and over again, even if everyone is replaced in the here and now. The patterns work to remind the organization about things that happened in the past and affect the culture and the people within the culture in the present day. To break through these patterns, the first event from the past that caused the patterns as an effect in the present day needs to be resolved. But how can you resolve an event from the past and the patterns in the here and now? This is where the 'lens' of Unity Conscious Leadership™ comes in.

A. Patterns Attract Patterns

If you have been working in an organization for a while, you will notice that if someone has left the company, over time the new colleague shows the same behaviours as his predecessor, without having known him or her. It is the pattern that attracts the new person to that position, and unconsciously influences those choosing the new person. That is, until the deep-rooted patterns in the organization and the person are resolved.

Culture evolves on an unconscious level which causes certain behaviours. The cause of these behaviours is not visible and is therefore difficult to change. By making the cause *visible* and looking for solutions, ways are opened to bring about change to the desired culture. The basis for researching, analysing and offering opportunities for change lies in information about events that have been taken place in the past.

From my experience, working on the soul level of the organization and people in the organization is the way to break through old pain and obstructing patterns. These are the triggers where the old pain and obstructing patterns start.

B. Facts About Cause and Effect of Cultural Dynamics

At Organizational level:

- Unjustified dismissal
- (family) Business succession
- Merger
- Reorganization
- Failure to recognize a founder or director.

At Work level:

- Power and influence structures
- Group norms
- Expectations
- Wishes
- Openness
- Trust
- Affective relationships between superiors and subordinates
- Dissatisfaction of employees with the organization and work.

At Personal level:

- Difficulty taking own place or feeling at home at the workplace
- Feeling rejected, excluded, not heard, not seen, invisible
- The feeling of not having found the right place
- The feeling that you can do things better than colleagues / managers
- Balance between giving and taking is disturbed
- Feeling insufficiently appreciated
- Having good ideas but nobody does anything with them

- Company accident or death within the organization
- Difficulty in taking responsibility
- Not daring to perform own tasks
- Afraid of making mistakes
- Lack of clarity about own competence, responsibilities and future opportunities
- Impeded competition between colleagues
- General uncertainty or dissatisfaction
- Repetitive conflicts
- Questions about career options
- Absence and staff turnover.

These occasions create an **undercurrent** within teams, departments and organizations...

And this creates in the here and now:

- Unrest
- Absenteeism
- High staff turnover
- Demotivation
- Conflict situations
- Power struggles
- Scapegoat mechanisms
- Resistance
- Fears
- Desires.

CHAPTER 7

UNITY CONSCIOUS LEADERSHIP™ CONCEPT OF CULTURAL TRANSFORMATION

When it comes to structure or culture,
culture will always win.
– Joyce Z. Wazirali –

My Experience on Cultural Level with CEOs as Culture Influencers

In my practice I also guide CEOs with their challenges about creating cultures on the condition that the CEO is also part of the cultural change process. Those who were open to making a deep personal change became my clients. The CEO and culture changed and was sustained.

I see many organizations struggling with advisors. They aim to work by persuading the owner to change the structure of the organization. For example, by changing from hierarchical model, (top down management) to a flat organisation (co-creation), leading the change process with more rules and regulations towards the staff members.

What happens tends to be chaos and imbalance. Staff members gets confused, burned-out, or sick. They make more mistakes and lose their common focus, aim and energy. They lose the connection with each other and with the clients, become lost in the jungle of rules and regulations, and then they may well resign. Clients who were accustomed to connecting with the staff members who have left the organization feel less or no connection with the organization. As a result, a decrease in the customer base occurs.

For me it is predictable that those things happen after changing the structure of the organization. To create a new culture the people, including the CEO are the most important aspect. If they start to connect in a genuine way with themselves and each other, the culture will change.

Connection from the perspective of *Unity Consciousness Leadership*™ means we acknowledge that we are *not* only a part of the culture, but also the *creators* of the culture. Whether it is a hierarchic or a flat organization, it's not about the form, it's about the perspective and attitude.

No matter if it is a hierarchic or a flat organization, culture is not about the structure. It is about the people in the organization and their perspectives, attitudes and interconnectedness.

The dynamic of the workplace is extremely complex. When we go to work, we all take our past, present and future with us and project it unconsciously onto each other. Past events and the blueprint of former employees are also stored in the collective memory of the organization and influence the employees in the here and now. Many people are influenced by the dynamic and a lot of potential gets lost or is not allowed to manifest.

By using obstacles at the workplace as a stepping-stone to growth and transformation and seeing tension as a motor for organization or team development, the culture will change and staff members will manifest their potentials for the benefit of the organization. *Can you imagine how the culture will change when everyone is allowed to use their potential?*

Unity Conscious Leadership™ Concept of Cultural Transformation

To change culture is not easy because of the complexity, as I will explain later.

Other culture influencers are decision makers, such as:

- Directors and managers
- Board members
- Supervisors and Commissioners
- Cooperation partners
- Care takers
- Teachers
- Parents
- Celebrities
- Government employees
- World leaders.

Unity Conscious Leadership™ Concept of Cultural Transformation

(According to my own experiences, insights, dream and visions)

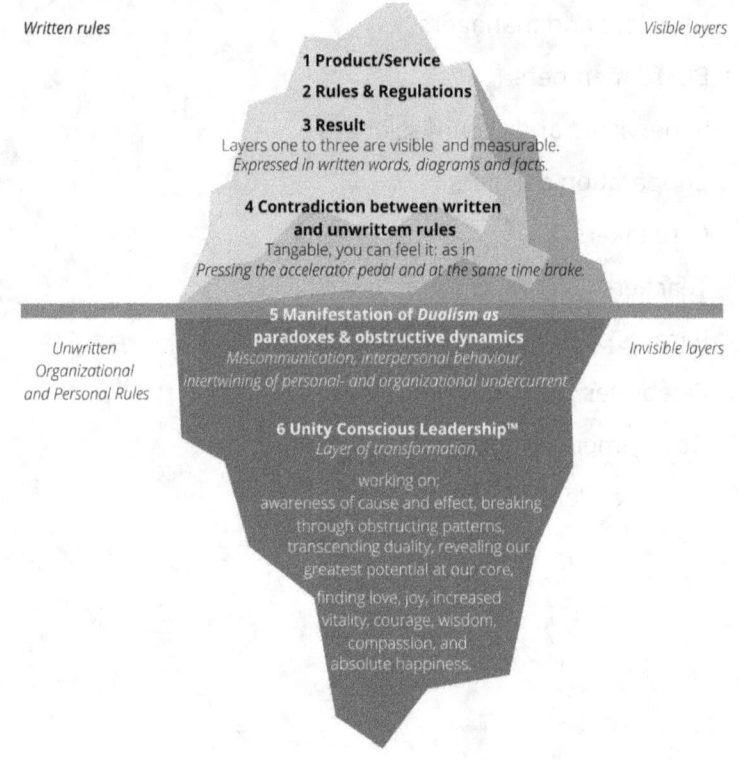

Concept of Cultural transformation (of *Joyce Z. Wazirali*)

Explanation of the Concept of Cultural Transformation

We monitor all the gates to change ourselves that can only be opened from the inside.

– Mary Ferguson –

A. Written rules

1. Layer one, product/ service

Organizations start with a purpose or mission, an aim to accomplish a product or service for the benefit of their clients and society. They articulate their mission and vision, as well as the resulting goals and strategies in words. Experience has shown that the business aims are often a few words on paper which have not been given sufficient meaning to. Everyone within the organization has their own interpretation of the company objective. As a result, they are not optimally achieving the business goals and there is a degree of miscommunication, creating a lack of; capacity, decisiveness, involvement and responsibility.

There are also organizations that have never recorded a mission on paper. Only the owner knows his or her goals, while the employees work on the production or the service.

Company K

The CEO and owner of Company K was facing problems in his organization in relation to how his staff performed their job. They were doing their job without thinking about how they presented themselves to their clients. Even though he corrected them regularly, he was not able to change the way they presented themselves. According to the CEO, the quality of their product and services was distinctive compared with that of his competitors. Therefore, it was important that his staff presented themselves in a distinctive way.

When I asked him about the mission of his company, he told me he didn't have one. That's the way they always worked, he said. He realized that he was the only one who knew what the goal of his company was. It was in his head, but not in the heads of his staff.

I guided a process of defining the company's vision, mission, goals, norms, values and beliefs together with the CEO and his staff. Everyone in the company was involved in this process. They formulated it together and at the presentation, staff members became aware of what they had done wrong in the past. It was as though they saw the company from a new perspective. They collectively agreed that quality, was not only about the quality of their product and services, but also about how they themselves performed. They had visions of previous summers when they had visited their clients in dirty cars, wearing short pants and showing hairy legs. Collectively, they agreed that their appearance was not representative of quality. They therefore decided to wear smart suits in the future and to wash their cars before going to see a client.

After this process, the CEO no longer had to correct his staff because they had adopted their own set of values and beliefs, which being collectively created, made it easy for them to attach meaning to.

2. Layer two, Rules and Regulations

This is the layer of formalization of agreements, appointments, profiles, contracts, working conditions, business procedures, etc.

3. Layer three, Result

On this layer all the results are gathered, presented and compared with the forecasts, such as the (interim) figures, income and costs, profit or loss, staff turnover, sickness absence, and action points to be taken.

B. Unwritten rules

The *unwritten rules* are the results of events and agreements from the past. They collectively influence the daily course of events in the present and future, until the causes from the past are resolved.

Influence of collective written and unwritten rules on behavior

Behaviour is a consequence of following *written and unwritten rules* within the organization and of the individuals in the organization. These rules continuously influence each other on an unconscious level.

Everyone who makes up the organization also takes not only their own *personal unwritten rules* to work, but also their experiences of unwritten rules from former workplaces. It happens on an unconscious level and evokes moods and feelings towards colleagues, which can create a *personal undercurrent*.

It is as though **the personal undercurrent confirms the organizational undercurrent and vice versa**. As a result, ratification of what has taken place in the past of the organization and the lives of people ensures that old pain and old *obstructing patterns* continue to repeat themselves within the organization and people themselves. This is despite the various efforts made to change things, including staff coaching and training and is reflected by constantly repeating obstructing patterns such as:

Obstructing patterns

- Difficulty in taking one's own place
- Restricting competition between colleagues
- General uncertainty
- Dissatisfaction
- Repeated conflicts
- Lack of clarity in leadership
- High absenteeism
- High staff turnover
- Repetitions of the same problem despite replacement of leadership

- Insufficient effect on education and training programmes
- Friction between different departments and subgroups within the organization
- Survival of old pains and other historical obstacles
- Lack of clarity about responsibilities
- General need for more decisiveness
- Customer loss or complaints
- Higher advisor and personnel costs
- Lower profit, or loss.

4. Layer four, Contradiction between written and unwritten rules

Layer four shows the tension field between layer one to three and layer five. Despite the action taken to improve the business result, things are still the same in the organization or even worse. The action undertaken did not contribute to improvement, worked only in the short term or the results became worse despite all the external guidance and training.

Meanwhile, the environment is changing, clients are more demanding, but nothing changes in relation to the future. Old pain and obstructing patterns act as a brake on the changes necessary for the future of the organization.

The contradictions are not only on the level of expected and actual behaviour, but also in terms of norms, values and beliefs.

Company A

The CEO and owner of company A had a company which delivered services to clients. During the previous three years, the company had incurred large losses after decades of flourishing and profit. The environment and the clients had been changing for years. The original customer base was mostly composed of older people, and as they died or moved to where they no longer needed the company's services, the CEO found it difficult to attract new and younger clients. Regardless of the various discounts, promotions and offers, the customer base kept decreasing and as a result, income was reduced while production costs remained the same.

The owner had discussed things with his accountant, who had recommended this action. But it did not succeed. The time for trial and error was over - something had to be done to turn the tide.

So the owner came to me because he knew me well and knew that I have a different perspective on how things work. I started to ask questions about his own attitude in the company and towards his clients. Soon he admitted that he had not been motivated for years and found it hard to move forward with his company. On the one hand he was forced to take steps towards the future but on the other, he lacked motivation to do so.

We worked on the underlying causes of his obstructing pattern which sabotaged the future of his business. Eventually, he felt motivated again and regained his strength. He attracted new and younger customers and his business started to grow again. Since then, the business has been profitable.

5. Layer five, Manifestation of Dualism

This layer is invisible, expressed as dynamics of perpetuating obstructing patterns and paradoxes. Perceptible with the senses but hard to grasp and comprehend. The dynamics and patterns are about miscommunication, interpersonal behaviour and the complexity of personal- and organizational undercurrent: caused by the dynamic of the three principles of:

- *Unity of person and environment,*
- *The Law of cause and effect, and*
- *The all-pervasive influence of the past, present and future in the here and now.*

(You can find the explanation of these three principles in chapter 2.)

Miscommunication

> **Encounters generate triggers,**
> **Triggers awaken memories,**
> **memories ignite emotions,**
> **emotions manifest feelings,**
> **feelings cause thoughts,**
> **thoughts become words,**
> **words become actions,**
> **actions create worlds.**
>
> – Joyce Z. Wazirali –

A. Mission Statement

As previously mentioned, communication in an organization starts with the defining and understanding of the mission and vision of the company. I once had a client who presented the mission statement of his company. The final lines of which were: 'we will fight the battle and win the war'. He asked me what I thought about it. I told him to skip the final lines, because; words create worlds. I also didn't see any connection between the final lines of battle and war with the business or clients.

A few weeks later, he presented the same mission statement including the final lines to his staff. And they were all clapping their hands and looked happy. It was as though I was in a different dimension. I did not understand their reaction.

After that, my client started a battle with his own staff. When he felt impotent, he just fired his own staff. Even people who had been working there for decades and did a good job.

B. "Pain" and "Wounds" From the Past

Miscommunication between colleagues can also end up in counteraction. A recurring pattern is also called "old pain". The origins may even have taken place 25 years ago. The people who were part of the origins of the "old pain" may well have already left the organization. And yet it still influences the employees in the organization in the present day.

Example
There was a team and team leader who I guided to work together again as one team. Over the years some miscommunications and "wounds" had arisen between employees and for those who had been working there for a long time, "old pain" kept coming back. With a few exceptions, the employees had chosen not to work together. On the other hand, if they were to serve their customers in an effective way, they had to cooperate.

But the 'old pain', miscommunication and 'wounds' created a blockage between the employees. As a result, work was being duplicated, production deteriorated, and customers were not well served.

First I worked with the team leader on a system dynamic level to get clear where the 'old pain' originally came from and to break through this pattern. The day after the session there was already a more positive atmosphere between the employees without them being aware of what had happened the day before.

The next week a 2-day team building workshop was planned. On the first morning, some employees refused to participate and reported sick, even though it was in their working time.

How can you do team building workshop if part of the team does not participate? The behaviour of the refusers was a reflection of their attitude and fears of the "confrontation" they wanted to avoid.

The team leader did everything to persuade the absentees to participate anyway. This time it was totally different, and they were tempted with pastries and tasty snacks.

We started the day on a positive note and soon compliments were being exchanged. There were employees who worried about what their colleagues would think of them and they therefore avoided contact with those colleagues. This is called "projection".

During the first morning, the team fell into the old pattern. A positive connection was made, but the negative connections in terms of "wounds", "old pain" and miscommunication had not been resolved. That was also part of my programme. I pushed this part forward.

Old pain was explained and forgiven in a respectful way. The team started to become a team again. An employee took the floor to praise me. He said that they had been given annual training for 25 years, each time with a different trainer who ran his or her own programme. I was the first trainer who had actually tuned into and made contact with the team. They felt seen and heard by me.

During the break the team decided to take a joint walk. This had never happened in the entire history of the team.

The rest of the training was very instructive and insightful for the whole team and the individual employees. The employees who initially reported sick were happy they joined the training despite their misgivings.

After the training, they changed their workplaces and sat in groups to work together. For the first time ever the production and profit of the team increased.

C. Adjusting ICT to the Abilities of the Employees

There was once an organization with which I was indirectly involved, but not to the extent that I knew all the ins and outs. I was struck by inconsistencies in the reports I saw, and I always got the feeling that they were cutting and pasting just to produce something. In retrospect, it became clear to me that the old and new ICT systems were being used at the same time. The old employees who refused to learn how to use the new system were allowed to use the outdated system. That way they were still available for work.

For years two different ICT systems were used. It would have cost the organization a lot of money to fire the stubborn employees, which is why the director opted for two systems instead of professional development. This created associated dangers regarding the quality and reliability of the reporting.

D. Not Communicating the Truth

An employee can leave the organization for various reasons. The reported reason does not always have to be the real reason. For example, a secretary who has had a secret affair with her boss may leave because it is a painful situation for her to be confronted day in day out with her boss and her ex-lover when the affair ends. Also, negative feelings of anger, fear, and jealousy often arise, which prevent cooperation. Because the affair was a secret, it is not discussed and to prevent anyone from finding out, the secretary closes herself off and thus feels lonely and used.

When she leaves, the next secretary will soon experience the same feeling of being excluded, while she likes to be in contact with her colleagues. For reasons she doesn't understand, she is not included in the team. On the other hand, her colleagues think, "Let's first see how long she stays before we connect with her." In the long term, their idea will become a self-fulfilling prophesy. And then they will conclude, "You see, it was predictable."

Interpersonal Behaviour and Patterns

Everywhere you meet people you can be triggered.

Feeling responsible

Once, a client came to me because she was burned out. She told me she woke up tired in the morning, was tired all day and during the night she also woke up a few times, often with thoughts about what she still had to do. She was working hard in her head while lying in her bed. The fatigue made her forgetful and slow, but she continued nonetheless.

She said "yes" to everything, even when a voice inside her called out very loudly "no." Her sense of responsibility was very strong, and it made her feel good if she could help people and receive compliments for it. Therefore, she often took on too much and then decided to work overtime. She struggled to set her limits, often did not know what her limits were, and had difficulty asking for help or indicating that it was all too much. Until her body refused.

She came to me and I guided her to find out where her great sense of responsibility came from. It was a pattern of taking responsibility, which she had known from childhood. As a result, she went beyond her own limits. We had worked on her childhood traumas and she could feel her own limits of responsibility again.

Finally she was able to feel and indicate her boundaries, say "no" without feeling guilty, and found she had more and more energy. When she returned to work, she realized that it was not the right place for her: her personal 'undercurrent' had changed and was a mismatch for that of the organization and workplace. She went to work for a different company, one where she enjoys working and gets energy from her work.

Being bullied

Another client had been bullied at school when he was a little boy. That was so long ago, he was barely aware of it anymore. Unknowingly it still had an influence on his life. In one way or another this pattern constantly repeated in his life. He often felt left out, unseen or unheard by friends, family and colleagues at work, and he seemed always to go to workplaces where his predecessor had been bullied.

Every time his childhood trauma of being bullied was triggered, it evoked sad feelings. When he resolved his trauma, his working environment changed in a positive way. He no longer felt invisible, and the feeling of being left out disappeared also.

Intertwining of Personal- and Organizational Undercurrent

This is complex to explain and is beyond the realms of this book. My intention is to evoke awareness of how Unity Conscious Leadership™

works. I will explain how this layer works, by giving some examples of experiences with directors of companies I have worked with.

***You have to co-operate,
before you co-create.***

– Joyce Z. Wazirali –

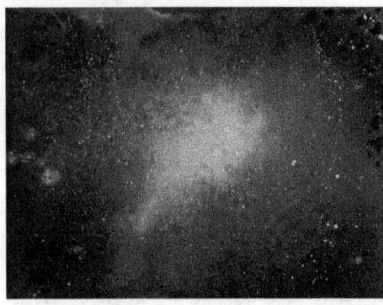

Co-creation is a new word which is expected to be easily achieved. In reality, it often turns out not to work. We try to realize co-creation through procedures. The focus is on achieving a goal such as production.

What is needed prior to co-creation is cooperation. Cooperation for our purpose is about the relationship between all individuals forming one team with a common aim or goal. The reasons why there may be problems with cooperation in workplaces are often: old pain, projection, prejudices, unfamiliarity, etc. These are elements that make people go out of connection.

We can compare teamwork with the human body. The body consists of various organs interconnected and influencing each other all the time. All organs have their unique tasks and talents. For the human body to function properly, there must first be good cooperation between the organs. If one organ refuses or functions less well, complaints arise on several levels such as physical, mental, emotional, social and spiritual pain or disorder.

Within a team, the cooperation is often invisible. What is visible is how the team members behave towards each other, what is being realized, what language is spoken, level of absenteeism, staff turnover, customer complaints and customer turnover.

For those who can perceive or feel the atmosphere in the room, the atmosphere provides extra information.

Organization XYZ

Organization XYZ consisted of various departments that had to work well together to deliver their services to their customers. The customers were often lost and complaining en masse.

During the investigation the real problem became clear. It turned out that two departments could not cooperate with each other for personal reasons of the various team members. The employees also suffered from old pains, an undercurrent of the organizational culture. As a result, they avoided contact with each other. Consequently, mistakes were made and there was no communication.

The interventions showed that the individual employees put themselves at the centre and projected their personal undercurrents onto each other. Rather than being focused on the organizational goal and the customers, they were focussing on each other.

The employees worked on their personal process and "old pain" between the departments, through coaching, counselling and workshops.

Since then, the employees of both departments have been working together in a pleasant way and customers are well served. The employees do far more work within the same time period than they were used to doing in the past, and the atmosphere has changed in a positive way. There is laughter and the employees of the departments are cooperating and co-creating together. They now have their joint focus on the customers and their mutual goals.

Company Q&A

Another client owned a company with 30 employees. They made unique products and had to keep innovating to retain their clients.

The owner was the only person responsible for innovation. He could not manage to work out his innovative ideas during office hours. For reasons he didn't understand, the workers were unable to work independently. Too often they were standing at his desk asking questions, which is why he chose to do his development work in the evening at home. This situation had been going on for years. By now his family had expanded and he didn't have time for them or himself. He knew it could not carry on that way, because it was at the expense of himself and his family. The only thing that would help would be his fellow workers standing on their own feet and being able to make decisions independently. Whatever he did, the situation did not change. He had already paid several consultants to solve the problem, but to no avail.

During our first interview, he asked what I did differently from the previous consultant. I replied that I didn't know because I had no idea what the previous consultant had done. He said he had written a thick report that had landed in his lower desk drawer. In the report, the consultant had merely repeated everything the owner had told him and suggested that he should continue with his existing plan. However of course, that did not answer the owner's question about what he should do differently. This adventure with the consultant had cost him a lot of time and money and had yielded nothing.

I told him that I am not too concerned with reports, but with interventions and actions. For that I needed his *time and personal involvement* because the problems could only be solved with us working together.

The questions I asked him in the first interview gave him so many new insights, which made him aware of the source of the problems he was struggling with. As a result, he decided to cooperate with me.

Firstly, I started working with the owner on finding out obstructing patterns within himself in order to resolve them using tailor-made interventions. Then I gave training to him and his employees. As they became aware of their joint mission, they became motivated and supported each other in several ways.

Some employees followed an individual personal development programme with me. During the process, the employees started to work more independently. The owner had time to devise and develop his innovative plans during working hours. He could finally spend his evenings with his family and make time for himself.

A while after my intervention, the company went through tough times due to changes with customers and the economy. Without any guidance, the owner led his organization independently through the crisis. Due to the sessions he had with me and what he had learned, he was able to make his own choices, no matter how difficult they were, to keep his company alive, something he had not been able to do before my guidance.

After the crisis, the company continued to flourish and remained successful.

We worked on his personal undercurrent and the undercurrent of his company and employees. That saved his company.

Company C

The owner had a company with around 40 employees with permanent and temporary employment contracts. He had not been happy with the functioning of his manager for a while, because the employees complained a lot about him. The owner was rarely present at his own company to witness the problems first-hand.

To solve the problem with the manager, the owner decided he should receive training. Despite this, the manager fell into his old patterns. A consultant was then hired to guide him. This effort was expensive and time-consuming, yet nothing changed.

I was the next consultant and indicated that I could only solve the problem with the cooperation of the owner. After all, my role is to clarify the cause of the problem and see where the key to the solution lies. The owner was completely open and cooperative. During my interviews it became clear that the owner could not really take his place as the business owner. So, he transferred his duties to the manager.

However, the owner also felt a degree of resistance when it came to taking his place and taking responsibility in his own company. He found the repetitive pattern of always saying goodbye to temporary employees particularly difficult. When he was about to go to the company for a farewell, something always happened that forced him to hand over the farewell ceremony to the manager. These were invariably the times when family crises arose. According to him, the fact that it happened that way was purely coincidental.

Not being able to say goodbye was a pattern for the owner himself. During an intervention it became clear that he had not said goodbye to a loved one at a very young age. This became not only a pattern in his life, but also a pattern in his company.

After working with him on his childhood trauma and breaking the pattern of not saying goodbye, he was able to take his place as the business owner. Since then, he has been able to deal with the farewell ceremonies himself. And because he could finally take his own place, the manager was no longer needed.

Layer Six, the Transformational Level

Cultural transformation can be realized through: awareness of the mechanisms behind current behaviour, use of the right interventions for cultural and personal development, establishing connection between employees by understanding the benefits of diversity and development of qualities, talents and inner strength for every person in the organization. Better cooperation arises through openness and propagation of the essence of the business goals.

Cultural transformation is too complex to explain in this book. Therefore, I will share some theory and practical examples from scientists whose insights gave the opportunity to develop interventions that work on personal and cultural level. Below I will share some brief information from several sources about 'the collective field' and 'system dynamic' perspective. In the reading list you will find recommended books on these topics.

A. The Collective Field

Lotus Sutra or Heart Sutra

In the Lotus Sutra they call it: the _entanglement of interconnectedness_ of people and their environment.

That is, cause and effect and past, present and future _in one single moment_.

Carl Gustav Jung

The _collective unconscious_ is a concept from the work of Carl Gustav Jung. According to his hypothesis, the collective unconscious is a *kind of storage place of latent images that humans have inherited as a species from their past.*

In fact, Jung's life's work focused on researching what was once "conscience" where we all seem to be in contact in a certain way. Newly born we are unaware of our collective unconsciousness, but the experience of every moment in the here and now helps us become aware of what was once known. It is conceivable that this conscience is not always correctly interpreted, because at this moment of evolution we are not yet able to bear our psychological totality.

Rupert Sheldrake

Rupert Sheldrake (b. June 1942) is an English doctor in cell biology and author of many books. He emphasizes the _collective conscious_ side of the field. As a biologist, he takes life as a starting point. From a human point of view there is a knowing field that everyone can become aware of. He sees it as a *universal energetic information centre*, to which life makes its contribution or draws on its knowledge. He emphasizes this biological function as the *seventh sense*, because it is not the same as having a sixth sense that we have in common with all animals and relates to intuition.

B. System Dynamics

Every person is part of multiple systems, such as the family of origin, the self-founded or compound family, sports club, friends club, colleagues, and so on.

Systems are again parts of larger systems. Just as a team is a part of a department, a department is a part of an organization and an organization is a part of society, and so forth.

We can also say that systems consist of subsystems. The sum of the subsystems is different from the system itself. In systems you come across patterns that keep repeating themselves. These patterns also occur in the subsystems.

For example, after the Salt March of India, the non-violent journey that started in 1930, Gandhi was fasting for days. He also had a spell in prison and was involved in other non-violent action together with the whole Indian population. During this time, all the people in India acted as one unit. Gandhi's leadership was instrumental in India eventually gaining its independence on August 15th, 1947. After the partition of India and Pakistan, violence started between Hindus and Muslims in India. We can see the Hindus and Muslims as the subsystems of India where the patterns that occurred right after the patterns of suppression by the British were solved, while during the suppression, the Hindus and Muslims lived in peace with each other united in a common cause.

The hundredth monkey

After the Second World War, a number of scientists conducted a study into the behaviour of Japanese macaques (monkeys) on the Japanese island of Kojima. The monkeys lived on different islands around Japan in different colonies. They ate potatoes that were thrown onto the beach. In the beginning the monkeys rushed to the beach. They took the potatoes and started to eat them. At one point the scientists found that on one island a few monkeys first washed the potatoes in the water before they ate them. As time went on, more and more monkeys on the same island started rinsing the potatoes before eating them. They were copying each other's behaviour.

Just as the hundredth monkey learned to wash the potatoes on *that* island, monkeys on the other islands began to wash their potatoes before they ate them. There was no communication, no contact between the islands. It was as if a critical number had to change their behaviour, so that it was suddenly taken over by the majority. And this all happened without the majority really having seen the practice. However, they had somehow become aware of it.

Improve the world, start with yourself

When people ask how they could ever possibly change this big world on their own, I find it's useful to talk about the story of the 100th monkey we mentioned earlier. You could be the hundredth monkey. You may well belong to that minority that indeed radically changes the behaviour and insights of others.

Only a small minority of serious devotees are needed to ensure that at a certain point the whole collective suddenly follows their example. In the history of the world there are plenty of examples of major changes brought about by a small group of highly dedicated people like Mahatma Gandhi, Nelson Mandela and so on.

Why Most Cultural Change Projects Fail

Cultural change is like *seeking a needle in a haystack* with many pitfalls. Such projects often fail because most projects are aimed at changing *behaviour* and *applying interventions from the perspective of Dualism*. They try to take away obstructing behaviour *(the effect)* and replacing it with *desired* behaviour. Trying to replace the *effect* is like looking in the mirror and camouflaging it so you can't see the pustules.

A. Team building

Within organizations people exhibit a certain behaviour and as an employer you organize team building days for better cooperation or team spirit. On the day itself it seems to go well and presents the illusion of the team being together. But once back in the workplace, the old familiar patterns of behaviour are repeated.

B. More procedures

Let us assume work is being done to improve procedures. And it also seems to encourage employees to work better together. Over time there seems to be some improvement with regard to work procedures but the relationship between employees is back to the old level and old patterns are starting to re-establish themselves, at all levels of the organization.

C. Replacing employees

Sometimes it is even decided to replace people in the workplace. Or to replace entire departments. There are advisers who recommend this strategy. After a while, everyone again shows the behaviour of their predecessors, without having known them. In the meantime, a culture of fear is being created within the organization and employees who have not been replaced get the feeling that they can be the next to leave.

With the departure of "old" employees, a lot of knowledge and potential is also lost. Employees who are passionate about the business are removed together with employees who perform less well. As a result, the organization is left without its 'bearing walls'.

D. Lack of personal development

The fact that employees perform less well is also due to the extent to which investments are made in professional and personal development. Often investments are only made in *professional* development in the form of seminars or training courses, rather than in the field of *personal* development.

E. Lack of professional development

In some organizations people suddenly find out that there are new developments. This may happen in the area of automatization, for example, when managers cannot avoid sending employees on a course. If nothing has been done for years about professional training, it is a big step for the older generation. They are then perceived as "not wanting to change or grow in their profession" or "looking forward to retirement in a few years."

F. Rapid change in ICT

It sometimes happens that several automatization systems are in use, old and new, to satisfy everyone's wishes. The automation of the *organization* is adapted to the employees instead of the *employees* to the automation in the perceived interest of the organization. This can have far-reaching consequences and higher costs within an organization. Using multiple automation systems is always more expensive than using one.

G. Burn out, obstructive patterns and undercurrent.

These are signals of an unhealthy organization. Sometimes it is difficult to fill certain positions in an organization. Occasionally one can find the desired person, or if someone has been appointed, over time he or she begins to demonstrate the same behaviour as the predecessor. As we have learned, patterns repeat themselves. The new employee struggles to be himself from the inside and yet fails. There is an "undercurrent" in the organization. The employee loses energy, is tired at the end of the day and has the feeling that he has worked very hard to stay with himself. As a result, the work demands a lot of energy and people get burned out.

The cause of people becoming burned out is often not only the undercurrent in the organization, but also how they deal with certain situations, each with its own "undercurrent".

Patterns attract patterns. There are patterns not only in the dynamics of behaviour within organizations. The employees also have their patterns that repeat themselves. These patterns are visible in the behaviour and certain feelings that repeat themselves.

The Complex of Personal and Organizational Dynamics

It is extremely complex to see through the dynamic of the invisible undercurrent, which is why professional knowledge and experience is required. Investments are often made in professional training and team building, which does not contribute to cultural development. Far too little is invested in breaking through obstructing patterns in the organization and personal development of individual employees. There is still a great deal to be gained from that.

One characteristic of patterns is that they keep repeating over time. Just like waves of the ocean. Whatever happens, the waves keep returning, sometimes higher, sometimes lower, depending upon prevailing circumstances.

How the waves arise is complex. One factor is the wind. It is tangible for us in that we feel it, but it is not visible. Another factor influencing the waves is the moon. And then there is a whole world moving beneath the waves. There are rocks in the water and undercurrent. They are all invisible and together influence the waves that *are* visible to us. This complexity also occurs in the dynamics of people and their behaviour. Often unconsciously.

The causes of the patterns are not visible. The resulting behaviour *is* visible, and it is often used to change behaviour because finding the underlying cause can simply be too difficult.

To be able to go back to the causes from the consequences, it is necessary to see through human behaviour and systems from the perspective of Unity Conscious Leadership™.

To change the patterns or rather break through, it is important to use self-reflection, and if needed, to get help from an experienced professional who can help you see things from the perspective of Unity Conscious Leadership™ or contact me by email; info@unityconsciousleadership.com or info@eenheidbewustleiderschap.nl.

Tips for Personal and Cultural Development

1. Eternally seeking personal development

Personal development through self-reflection is also a principle of the Lotus Sutra (Nichiren Buddhism). It is not an easy way but is a profound way to grow and evolve as a human being.

People in organizations and their environment trigger each other unconsciously all the time, creating patterns in behaviour and movement. These patterns attract each other like magnets. The people attract the organization, and the organization attracts the people. To break the patterns of one it is essential to break through the patterns of both. So, it is not just organizational development but also the development of the people who create the organization. That is often forgotten. If you want to break the patterns, you have to break the patterns on both sides.

2. Use tension or crisis for growth

Often where people work in a team, there is tension between them. Because of the tension, people start to avoid each other. What happens next is that co-operation stagnates, which affects the organizational goals.

For example, once I had a client who was frequently fired by various companies. This was a pattern in her work life for many years and she wanted to break this pattern.

From the perspective of Unity Conscious Leadership ™ we used her previous workplaces as a mirror of her inner world. We discovered a common thread of conflict with her supervisors. For some reason she assumed that she was better than them and they triggered her in a negative way.

Together we investigated that pattern in multiple life areas such as family, friends, and leisure activities. Everywhere she assumed herself better than others.

She was the eldest child in the family and this pattern started when her baby brother was born. Her parents did not give her so much attention anymore and she decided to act as if she was a parent for her baby brother to get their attention back. Her parents praised her caring attitude and how she behaved in such a mature way towards her brother.

In terms of system dynamics, she had left her place as a child and took a new place as equivalent to her parents. Over the years she developed an attitude of not tolerating authority.

The cause of her trigger towards her supervisors was the trauma of feeling left out by her parents since the birth of her brother and taking another position in the family system. She realized she had been projecting her childhood trauma not only onto her supervisors but also her parents, brother and friends.

We did an intervention to step back into her own place as the daughter of her parents and sister of her brother. She felt relieved about not having the responsibility of carrying the burdens of her parents anymore. Since then, her relationships in all life areas have changed in a positive way. Authority is not a trigger for her anymore. She stayed at the same company and gained promotion.

By using tension or crisis as a counsellor for personal and group development, growth and transformation will take place on both sides, the people and organization. That is because the people and organization are one, entangled with each other. Change or transformation on a personal level will influence the group dynamic in a positive way and vice versa.

Unity Conscious Leadership™ for interdependent growth and transformation is a new paradigm on leadership for more health, happiness and peace. With the belief that we are all interconnected, interdependent and continuous influencing each other, we can *overcome and transform crises for personal, cultural & professional growth.*

3. Unlock potential on multiple levels

A. Combine organizational *and* personal development

When change processes within organizations run alongside change processes of individual employees in the area of personal development, a synergy effect is created whereby both the organization *and* the individuals experience a growth in potential. Both get into a flow, people extract energy from their work, radiate energy and thereby become ambassadors for the organization.

That was one of the success factors at the Plasa Group[11] and my clients who had been open to working from the perspective of Unity Conscious Leadership™ for the past three decades.

B. Align personal- and organizational mission

> *The key to creating true passion,*
> *is discovering*
> *your true talents*
> *and your purpose in life.*
>
> – Aristotle –

The organization and people who make up the organization have a mission for which they have been given talents, which enable them to achieve that mission. If the organization mission is clear and everyone can contribute their own life purpose and talents to accomplish their personal and common aim, the organization and the people will thrive, becoming healthy and adaptable to change.

For example: when someone has a personal mission to help suffering people and make them healthy and happy again, a job at a healthcare organization will make it possible to contribute his or her passion to, and align with, the mission of the organization. Working as a car salesman would not contribute or align, as there would be no passion.

C. Foster personal leadership

The prerequisite for a successful organization is to have resilient, healthy and happy employees.

---

[11] From 1988 to 2001, Joyce Z. Wazirali was co-founder, CEO and HR-manager of the Plasa Group, a company providing business services, which started with two founders. Within 13 years the Plasa Group grew into a company with various departments and 80 employees. Their customers and employees were their greatest ambassadors.

People who know their talents and life mission and can deploy them in their lives are more resilient, healthier and feel happier. Peoples' talents are their innate potential, give colour to who they are at their core, and represent the building blocks of their (life) mission. The more people are aware of that and put it into practice, the easier it becomes to do the things that come easily and gives them energy and make their inner leadership grow.

The more organizations allow their employees to operate their own leadership, the more the joint potential and mission will grow and contribute to connection, better cooperation, harmony, a pleasant (working) atmosphere and a healthy organization.

4. Embracing diversity/ transcending differences

In Nichiren Buddhism there is a profound principle, for which they have a special term - '**Itai Doshin**'. Which means, **the Unity of 'many in body one in mind.'**

'Many in body,' also translated as 'different in body,' refers to the diversity among individuals—their unique personalities, talents, qualities, abilities and roles.

'One in mind'—also 'same mind' or 'same heart'—means sharing a noble purpose, a common wish to realize a lofty goal.

The unity of many in body, one in mind can be formed only among those who respect one another and cherish one another's unique attributes and abilities, while working in harmony to compensate for one another's weaknesses. To create this kind of unity, each person must set aside attachment to self and accomplish a profound inner transformation. In Buddhism we call it **human revolution**.

'Human revolution' is a never-ending process of continual self-improvement. It describes a Buddhist way of life that eternally seeks growth and personal development. It is about how much we are growing and improving right now rather than what we have achieved in the past.

It also means **transcending mutual differences** to achieve a common goal.

Some associate the word 'unity' with conformity, and hence view it as being negative. Unity that is forced and seeks to control people, however, is the complete opposite of the unity of 'many in body, one in mind'. That might best be described as "one in body, different in mind". The more people are coerced to conformity, the less able they will be to genuinely unite in spirit. Under such circumstances, people may put on a show of unity but are in reality more concerned with protecting their own interests.

5. Use obstacles as a springboard for growth

> *Surfers use high waves for surfing,*
> *mountaineers use mountains to reach the top.*
>
> – Daisaku Ikeda –

Often obstacles are seen as barriers to achievement, or as objects we must find ways to get around. In reality, there are times when they can be useful and good. It also happens that the same or similar obstacles keeps arising. By always doing the same thing you always did, you will get the same thing you always got. The solution can usually be found within the person who suffers from the problem. Many people have to deal with the problem of where to find the solution, and how difficulties can be solved. Because *every person* and every situation is unique, there are no standard solutions.

The Keys to the Solutions

The higher someone stands on the ladder of hierarchy, the more their thoughts, words and actions will influence the cultural dynamic.

The most influential and responsible people in organizations are the role models. They are the main keys to the solutions. When we talk about culture, we often think of organizations. Culture exists in various systems where people are joined together because of their birth or collective aim.

Other role models are:
parents, (composite) family, board members, supervisory or commissary board, collaborative partners, care providers, teachers, celebrities, government and world leaders.

An open and vulnerable attitude on their part is necessary to make a sustainable change possible.

Anyone who wants a profound change and dares to be open and accessible is always welcome to contact me by email:
info@unityconsciousleadership.com or
info@eenheidbewustleiderschap.nl.

Eight Steps for Cultural Change with Unity Conscious Leadership™

1. System dynamic perception

Obtain awareness of interconnectedness and interdependence of people, organizations and environments.

2. Trigger(s) and patterns

Find the trigger(s) of the shift in the order in the system. For example, as a reaction to a trigger, people suddenly get sick, resign, and clients start complaining, etc.

Ask yourself: *what happened right before the shift and is there a pattern?* Discover the patterns in the system and the subsystem. For example, what are the patterns of departments, clients, suppliers, etc.

3. Cause and effect

Find out what could have happened in the past (that could even be yesterday) to cause this dynamic. You can use the list of facts about cause and effect of cultural dynamics in chapter 6.

4. Paradoxes

Find the undercurrent in the culture. You can use the list of examples of paradoxes and behaviour in organizations in Chapter 1.

5. Self-Reflection

Start with your own reflection, observing your own contribution to the situation. Mirror the paradoxes you have found with the patterns in your own life or inner world. You can use the list of examples of patterns and behaviour on personal level in Chapter 1.

6. Introspection

Take the insights of your reflection for introspection. Ask yourself, *when did I experience this before?*

7. Transform through Unity Conscious Leadership™

Find a qualified professional who understands and practices Unity Conscious Leadership™ in his or her own life, and understands how system dynamics work to apply the right intervention to your problem or contact me via my website www.unityconsciousleadership.com or www.eenheidbewustleiderschap.nl.

8. Make it generative

Take the insights you get from the transformation and share your experience with others who could benefit from it.

Unity Conscious Leadership™ Concept of Cultural Transformation

PROFESSIONAL LEADERSHIP

CHAPTER 8

THE TRUTH BEHIND THE FACTS

*Compassion is
the keen awareness of
the interdependence
of all things.*
– Antoine de Saint-Exupéry, The Little Prince –

Discovering the Truth Behind the Facts

Stairway to transformation

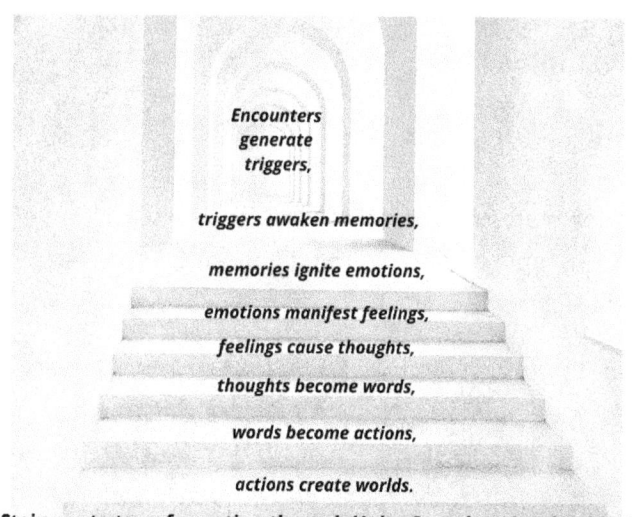

Stairway to transformation through Unity Conscious Leadership™

If you want to create a healthy, happy and peaceful world, take the steps back to where your trigger started. Take a deep dive into your own inner world and discover the beautiful *jewel* representing your hidden potential to create a new world.

Facts are not truths

We all are witnesses of events happening to us, in our environment and the world. What we experience is an event which is an outcome of the truth. The truth is invisible. To find the truth behind the event is only possible with an attitude of openness and without judgments, but with interconnectedness, transcending differences and heart to heart dialogue.

The Power of Dialogue

Dialogue is the way to make heart to heart connections. There you will find the truth and absolute happiness.

Practical examples

Mike

In 2001, 13 years after the establishment and construction of the Plasa Group with 80 employees, when I said goodbye, I received a card from Mike, which I still have.

He wrote: *Joyce, through this card I want to thank you for everything you have done for me. Thank you for the confidence you have had in me and for making me so sure of myself. The photo on the right reminds me of one of the best days of my life. Have fun with Eric and Amy and I will never forget your wise words:*

The Truth Behind the Facts

'You can't run away from yourself'

Thank you, Joyce, for the best time of my life.

Lots of love, Mike.

The secret of Mike (it is not his real name)

I had hired Mike when he was a young man. During our job interview I noticed that he was uncertain. Without any information about his history, it was clear to me that he had experienced something serious in his life. I also saw a lot of potential in Mike and had given him the opportunity to grow at his own pace.

He was given more extensive tasks more slowly than usual until he was able to fully function. The process had taken several years.

His uncertainty became less and less and I saw a deeper layer emerge behind his uncertainty. I couldn't give words to it. It was as if the real truth was hidden behind his uncertainty.

When he was finally able to do his job independently and efficiently, he came to submit his resignation.

I told him sincerely what I had observed with him through the years. He displayed a pattern of running away from his personal happiness. Every time he felt happy, he did something to avoid that feeling. The only thing I wished him was to enjoy that feeling of happiness.

He started to cry. I didn't need to know what he had been through. I gave him a few days' paid leave to sort things out for himself. In the end I said to him: *you cannot run away from yourself.*

He thanked me warmly and stayed home for two days. When he came back to work, he said that the conversation with me had hit to the very heart of his problem. He also had to convey the gratitude of his parents to me. Something that no other therapists or his parents had succeeded in was resolved through the conversation with me.

I was not aware of what I had done other than speaking to him from my heart and wishing him all the best.

It turned out that at a very young age he became unhappy due to a traumatic event and had been taking a pill every day for years to get closer to his sense of happiness.

After our conversation and the insight he received, he stopped looking for happiness outside himself. He could regain his own happiness and no longer needed the pills. He decided to continue working at the Plasa Group.

Joan

Joan was hired by my business partner. As the person ultimately responsible for the well-being of all employees, I discovered a pattern in Joan's behaviour.

Joan reported sick every three weeks and came back to work fresh and fruity a week later. It struck me that she had no evidence of being sick at all, and when she returned after her sick leave, she looked like she had been on holiday.

Because of this pattern, she burdened her other colleagues with extra work and they could not rely on her contribution.

One day I confronted her with my observation.

Firstly, she was struggling and insisted that she was really ill. I said that that was not credible given her appearance, and that I felt there was another story behind her reports of illness.

Then she agreed that I was right and told me that she came to work at the Plasa Group because her boyfriend wanted her to. But she was not happy with her job because she preferred to work in a larger work environment where she did not stand out and was just one of many. I told her that the real reason was not the size of the company. These were all excuses outside of herself.

When I asked her more questions, she concluded that she had done everything to meet her boyfriend's requests, so he could be happy with her. She had even chosen her field of study for him. Not because her talents were there. That's why the work cost her a lot of energy and wore her out, and she needed time to recover after a while.

I advised her to do things that made use of her talents, as that would give her energy and make her happy. Also, I explained that her boyfriend's happiness did not depend on what she did or didn't do, and that she was responsible for her own happiness, not his.

Joan thanked me for the conversation and the insights she had received. She resigned the same day to manifest her own happiness.

My Legacy from the Plasa Group

I define divine love as
the will to expand itself with the aim
of nurturing one's own or others spiritual growth.

– M. Scott Peck –

During my time at the Plasa Group, as co-founder, CEO, HR manager and co-builder of a big family, I had my own inner state of being.

1. I was aware of the invisible intelligence of the Universe, our interconnectedness, and how we all influence each other with our past, present and future. I knew I was a part of a bigger system.

2. I was always in a learning state through education and experiences on several levels.

3. I was feeling the responsibility for the happiness of everyone in the company and our clients, including my own.

4. Every day I started by looking to myself and everyone as if it were for the first time, with no judgment or reference to their past. Like a baby opening his eyes for the first time in life, looking at the world in wonder.

5. I gave everyone a place in my heart. Even though I knew that sometimes some staff members were not honest or suffering their own pain in their hearts. The truth was revealed after a while in many different ways. I see these as lessons *I* had to learn to grow and transform *myself*. So, thank you for the lessons.

6. I was genuinely loving and interested in everyone. Every morning I went to say good morning to my staff members and have a brief chat to sense if they were alright or needed any help on a personal or professional level.

7. That opened my heart to seeing their struggles and their potential. The staff members trusted me, and I was their personal guide equipped with tools for personal leadership. Many told me secrets I have never shared with anyone. Not even with my business partners.

8. If I felt or experienced a situation of disorder, I engaged in self-reflection to find out what I should change in myself or in the organization to the benefit of the whole organization and our clients.

9. I focussed on the interrelationship and interdependence of everyone in the whole system and beyond, that unfolded as patterns and paradoxes in my awareness.

10. That made the dynamic of the systems of every individual, our organization and clients visible to me, and thus, I took action.

11. If it was me creating the pattern, I worked on my personal leadership. If it was someone else, I talked to them, made them aware of their influence on the situation and guided them into their personal leadership.

12. Every time I felt disorder, I knew that the system was out of balance and by intervening, order in the organization could be re-established.

Traits and Mastery

The great task of leadership is
to create alignment of strength,
making our weaknesses irrelevant.

– Peter Drucker –

For me Mahatma Gandhi and Nelson Mandela are great examples of Unity Conscious Leadership™.

Nelson Mandela studied Mahatma Gandhi's traits during his detention. He had also studied his chosen words, norms, values and beliefs, and learned how to forgive. Both used nonviolent communication and were role models for many people.

1. Traits of Unity Conscious Leadership™

- Aware of being a role model
- Aware of their influence on their environment
- Always working on their own personal development
- Fearless; think, talk and act in Unity
- Genuinely loving, caring and peaceful
- Empathetic
- Connecting
- Inspiring
- Curious
- Patient
- Good observer, listener and advisor
- Read and listen between the lines
- Persistent
- Resilient and Adaptable to change
- Non-judgemental
- Focussed on equality despite grades and positions
- Transcends mutual differences.

2. Personal Mastery

- A person who takes responsibility for his own actions, is aware of the effect of his thoughts, words and deeds upon himself, his environment and everyone and everything involved within the short and long term
- An appreciative person aware that he's a part of the interconnectedness
- Who is aware of his environment as a mirror of his inner world

- Uses the opportunities of obstructing feelings in an interdependent relationship (visible or in thoughts) for self-reflection, self-inspection and self-development
- Integration and mastery of Unity Conscious Leadership™ in daily life
- Awareness of own reflection on environment
- Continually working on own personal development
- Speaking from the heart or nonviolent communication.

3. Cultural Mastery

- Observe with a System Dynamic perspective
- A continuous process of shaping a culture where everyone can use personal development, letting the potential of the individuals and total system grow and be used
- A culture of safety, integrity, connectedness, openness and trust
- Aware of interconnectedness and interdependence with environment, stakeholders and clients and vice versa
- Aware of the human behaviour strategy
- Unlock potential and embrace diversity
- Use dialogue to communicate
- Use obstacles as a springboard for growth
- Use tension or crisis as a counsellor for personal and group development
- See his own role in the culture
- Can see hidden potential in the people and organization
- Steer cooperation and co-creation
- Appreciative attitude and example

- The ability to connect people
- Creator of an environment where potentials can flourish
- Knowing that everyone has their unique talents and role
- Creates resilience and adaptability to change systems
- Creates a healthy, happy and peaceful world.

4. Professional Mastery

- Leading with the awareness of Unity Conscious Leadership™
- Possessing traits of Unity Conscious Leadership™
- Have integrated and practicing Personal and Cultural Mastery.

The Truth Behind the Facts

LAST BUT NOT LEAST

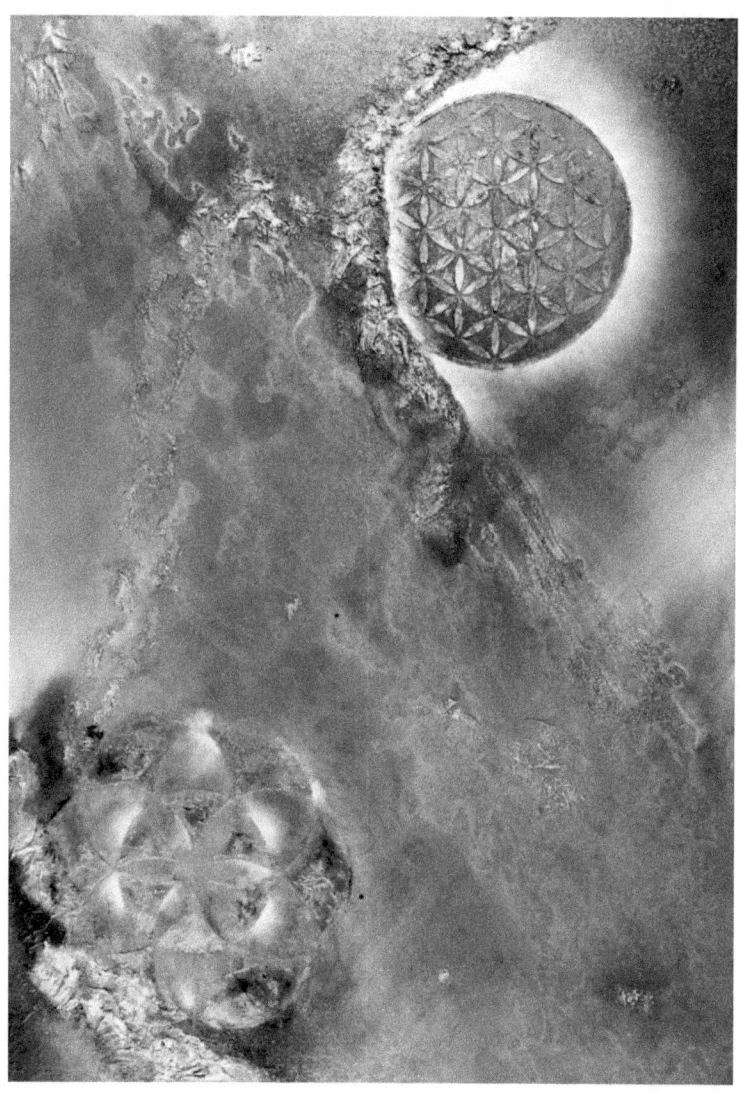

CHAPTER 9

LAST BUT NOT LEAST

You can't run away from yourself

– Joyce Z. Wazirali –

Revealing our Diamond

*Knowing your own darkness
is the best method for
dealing with
the darkness of other people.*

– Carl G. Jung –

The shadow is simply the dark side of someone's personality. And what is dark is always known only indirectly through projection. That is how, one discovers his dark side as something belonging to others: friends, relatives, fictitious characters, etc. This is why the meeting with the personal shadow is considered to be a moral effort. The difficulty integrating the shadow is huge if we have to face this powerful figure alone.

The parable of the jewel in the robe (Lotus Sutra)

A poor man went to visit a good friend. He was soon drunk and fell asleep. Before he left for a business trip, his good friend had sewn a very precious jewel in the lining of the poor man's robe.

When the man woke up, he resumed his life like a wanderer, completely ignorant of his precious jewel in his robe. Over the years he became more and more destitute.

One day he ran into his good friend. His friend was surprised to know that this poor man was getting poorer. The friend showed him the jewel that he had sewn into his robe. When the poor man discovered the jewel, he was in 'seventh' heaven! He was relieved of poverty, thanks to the gifted jewel.

Insight

The good friend is your own soul, and the poor man is an ordinary person. The jewel is the 'diamond' that is present in everyone who starts to shine more and more as people look for answers and solutions within themselves. Or the seed that is in everyone, that will only start growing and flowering if you focus your attention on it.

Transformation

The Myth of the Phoenix

The morning after I finished the final chapter, I woke up with a vision of the Phoenix.

According to the story, the Phoenix was a mythical bird with red and yellow feathers, which allegedly lived in Arabia. It lived on the tree of lore on Qaf mountain which was next to the seven valleys. Their names were reputed to be: **Wish, Love, Skill, Exception, Oneness, Surprise,** and **Absence,** although these seem to vary depending on the version of story.

In a lot of civilizations, the Phoenix has a different meaning: In China, *Rokh*, In Arabia, *Anka,* In Persia, *Simurg*, and in Turkey *Tugrul*.

The most famous characteristic of the bird was its ability to resurrect. Thus, it represents a cyclical process from death to life. People believed that one touch of its tears and wings was therapeutic.

The Phoenix rose from its ashes every 500 years after burning itself. From the pile of ashes, a new phoenix was born, one that gathered the remaining ashes of the bird that preceded it.

The Phoenix is up to this day a universal symbol of rebirth and the beginning of a new cycle.

It was believed that the Phoenix was a bird which never settled on the land and its feet never touched the land throughout its life. And it used to fly so high that it was not seen by anybody.

There is a saying in English literature:

'To rise like a Phoenix from the ashes.'

Meaning:

'To be powerful and successful again.'

This is what I **wish** for everyone who reads this book;

- To come closer to absolute **love**
- To use the **skills** we have been given
- To know we are all **exceptional**

- To live in **Oneness**
- To see the world *in wonder* like a newly born child
- With complete *absence* of (previous) conditioning
- Let the **inner sun shine brighter** every day.

Somewhere deep inside we all have a Phoenix.

Future Leadership

Unity Conscious leadership™

The collective crisis **caused** by the pandemic is a traumatic experience for many people and businesses worldwide.

After the pandemic and social distancing, when everything comes to a new normal, a lot of work will need to be done to resolve the **effects** of this crisis.

Therefore the opportunity arises to *make a fundamental change* in leadership and reconnecting with each other.

Unity Conscious Leadership™ provides a new paradigm on leadership, not only to resolve the effects, but also to eternally practice connecting from heart to heart with each other, and to *rise like a phoenix from the ashes*.

Reference list/reading list:

The Lotus Sutra

Peaceful Action, Open Heart: Lessons from the Lotus Sutra
Thich Nhat Hanh, Paralax Press 2009

The Living Buddha: An Interpretive Biography (Soka Gakkai History of Buddhism),
Daisaku Ikeda, Middleway Press 2008

Creating the Culture of Peace: A Clarion Call for Individual and Collective Transformation,
Anwarul K. Chowdhury, Daisaku Ikeda, I B Tauris 2018

The Buddha in Your Mirror: Practical Buddhism and the Search for Self,
Woody Hochswender, Greg Martin & Ted Morino, Middleway 2001
More books of explanation about the Lotus Sutra,
http://www.nichirenlibrary.org/

More information available on the websites:
https://www.daisakuikeda.org/
https://www.sokaglobal.org

The Collective Field

The Metamorphosis of Plants,
Johann Wolfgang von Goethe & Gordon L. Miller, Bio Dynamic Farming, 2004

Wholeness and the Implicate Order,

David Bohm, Routledge 2002

The Archetypes and the Collective Unconscious,
Jung Carl Gustav Jung, Routledge 1991

The Undiscovered Self,
Jung Carl Gustav Jung, Routledge 2013

Unified Field Theory: a new interpretation,
Albert Einstein, Sunrise 2017

Morphic Resonance: The Nature of Formative Causation,
Rupert Sheldrake, Parkstreet Press 2009

The Presence of the Past: Morphic Resonance and the Memory of Nature,
Rupert Sheldrake, Icon Press 2011

The Field: The Quest for the Secret Force of the Universe,
Lynne McTaggart, Element 2003

Quantum physics

You Are the Universe: Discovering Your Cosmic Self and Why It Matters,
Deepak Chopra M.D. & Menas C. Kafatos Ph.D., Rider 2018

Organizational

Liberating the Corporate Soul: Building a Visionary Organization,
Richard Barrett, 0-7506-7071-1

Complex Responsive Processes in Organizations: Learning and Knowledge Creation,
Ralph D. Stacey, Routledge 2001

Experiencing Risk, Spontaneity and Improvisation in Organizational Life; Working Live,
Patricia Shaw & Ralph Stacey, Routledge 2005

Good to great: Why some companies make a leap... and others don't,
Jim Collins, Random House 2001

Managing Oneself,
Peter F. Drucker, Harvard Business Reviews 2017

Other

Self-Renewal: the Individual and the Innovative Society
John W. Gardner, W.W. Norton and Co. 1996

The Awakening of Intelligence,
Jiddu Krishnamurti, 978-0060648343 Harper San Francisco 1997

Think on These Things,
Jiddu Krishnamurti, Harper San Francisco 1997

NOVA - The Miracle of Life (Video),
Lennart-Nilsson
Studio: WGBH Boston PBS, DVD, available at;
https://www.amazon.com/Nova-Miracle-Life-Lennart-Nilsson/dp/6302895189

Emotional Intelligence: Why It Can Matter More Than IQ
Daniel Goleman, Bloomsbury 1996

Left to Tell: Discovering God Amidst the Rwandan Holocaust
Immaculée Ilibagiza, Hayhouse 2014

Mohandas K. Gandhi, Autobiography: The Story of My Experiments with Truth,
Mohandas Karamchand Gandhi & Mahatma Gandhi, Penguin Classics 2001

Long Walk to Freedom: The Autobiography of Nelson Mandela,
Nelson Mandela, Abacus 1995

Heart Intelligence: Connecting with the Intuitive Guidance of the Heart,
Doc Childre, Howard Martin, Deborah Rozman & Rollin McCraty, Waterfront Press 2016

The Little Prince,
Antoine de Saint-Exupéry, Macmillan 2020. Plus many other options.

About the Author

We are the creators of our own world.
We can change our world
by using the triggers
we encounter in life
for self-refection, self-inspection and self-development
from the perspective of Unity Conscious Leadership™.

– Joyce Z. Wazirali –

Joyce Z. Wazirali is an author and universal consultant, coach, counsellor, speaker and trainer for people and business. For over 30 years, she has specialized in Unity Conscious Leadership™. She is also an artist and illustrator.

After six years working as a clinical chemical analyst at a hospital, she became an entrepreneur and started her own business in 1988. Since then, she has increased her knowledge and understanding through education[12] and experience in building a successful organization, personnel and personal

---

[12] Educations; Clinical Chemical Analyst, Payroll Administration, Egyptian Cartouche Master, Certifying Accountant, Basic Medical Knowledge, NLP Trainer, Systemic-dynamic constellations with families- and organizational systems, Work and Organizational Psychology, process guidance / facilitator for self-managing teams, learning organizations and organizational development, Appreciative Inquiry (Hasselt University, Leuven, Cleveland Ohio), certified core quadrant trainer, certified talent coach.

development, complex business processes, system dynamics of people and organizations and HR (human resource management).

In 1988 she became Director and one of two co-founders of a successful company in business services, which grew in 13 years to a company with 80 staff members.

For six years, she was chair of the audit committee on a supervisory board for 600 general practitioners.

With her company Unity Conscious Leadership™, she focusses on solving problems that hold people and organizations in the past, helping them develop their strength in the present and reveal opportunities for the future.

She offers face-to-face and online, tailor-made personal and group programs for:

- Unity Conscious Personal Leadership™
- Unity Conscious Cultural Leadership™
- Unity Conscious Professional Leadership™
- System-dynamic counselling for family systems
- System-dynamic counselling for teams and organizations
- Appreciative Inquiry (AI) summits
- Inner journey to one's talents and life mission
- Trauma therapy.

Her roots are in Asia, South America and Europe. The combination of Eastern descent, Southern temperament and Western upbringing, and growing up in many cultures has made her a versatile person. She has a holistic view of life, looking for causes and solutions within herself. The combination of connection with nature and her environment, study, Kriya yoga, Nichiren Buddhism (universal philosophy of life), sport, self-reflection and giving meaning to life helps her to get closer to her own nature.

In her practice Unity Conscious Leadership™, she works at rational-, physical-, social-emotional-, spiritual- and soul levels.

Her vision is:

'man is a unique and versatile creature, with deep answers for a healthy, happy and peaceful life.'

For more information, visit her on:

Websites	: www.unityconsciousleadership.com or www.eenheidbewustleiderschap.nl
Facebook	: https://www.facebook.com/UnityConsciousLeadership
LinkedIn	: https://www.linkedin.com/in/joyce-z-wazirali-3b70265/
YouTube	: https://YouTube.com/c/UnityConsciousLeadership

What clients say

'An inner change in the life of a single individual can bring a change in the lives of countless others and ultimately change the entire world'

– Josei Toda –

"The process through which Joyce takes you is unique, a wonderful recognition and discovery. About yourself and your environment and the reasons why things have developed. As they have the quest for clarity, it cannot be done alone. You need someone to help with this, someone with integrity and who "knows" what is going on without judging. Precognitive ability from an exceptionally strong intuitive ability. Joyce excels at this. But she is also humble, with a light step on the ground and a feeling for your often unconscious reality. "

– Martien van der Velde, Business Economist, Teacher, The Netherlands

"Thanks to your input, I am able to get a stalled group of people moving again. You are able to let people look at others with a positive outlook in order to continue with each other from there."

– Bob Brinks, Municipality of Helmond, The Netherlands

"It is very pleasant and enjoyable to be with you. I am extremely satisfied with the result. I certainly had my doubts in the beginning. I didn't really believe in it, now I can say that the insights you gave me in our first conversation were just right and turned out to be true. "
"It is especially good to hold up a mirror to oneself and get to know oneself. This ensures that others also align more with you. As a CEO, you gather people around you who want to go in the same direction, this happens without using words. Especially if you feel stuck and do not know what to do, it is recommended to talk to Joyce."

– Patrick van Ham, CEO at van Ham Exclusive.com, The Netherlands

Other Books Published by Make Your Mark Global

Holistic Healing
Created and Compiled by Andrea Pennington

The Top 10 Traits of Highly Resilient People
Created and Compiled by Andrea Pennington

The Real Self Love Handbook: A Proven 5-step Process to Liberate Your Authentic Self, Build Resilience and Live and Epic Life
by Andrea Pennington

Magic and Miracles
Created and Compiled by Andrea Pennington

Life After Trauma
Created and Compiled by Andrea Pennington

The Magical Unfolding by Helen Rebello

The Orgasm Prescription for Women
by Andrea Pennington

Time to Rise
Created and Compiled by Andrea Pennington

SMILER Can Change it All
by Gegga Birgis

The Book on Quantum Leaps for Leaders: The Practical Guide to Becoming a More Efficient and Effective Leader from the Inside Out
by Bitta. R. Wiese

Turning Points
Compiled and Edited by Andrea Pennington

Daily Compassion Meditation: 21 Guided Meditations, Quotes and Images to Inspire Love, Joy and Peace
by Andrea Pennington

Eat to Live: Protect Your Body + Brain + Beauty with Food
by Andrea Pennington

MAKE YOUR MARK GLOBAL

Get Published Share Your Message with the World

Make Your Mark Global is a branding, marketing and media agency based in the USA and French Riviera. We offer publishing, content development, and promotional services to heart-based, conscious authors who wish to have a lasting impact through the sharing and distribution of their transformative message. We also help authors build a strong online media presence and platform for greater visibility and provide speaker training.

If you'd like help writing, publishing, or promoting your book, or if you'd like to co-author a collaborative book, visit us online or call for a free consultation.

Visit www.MakeYourMarkGlobal.com

Call +1 (707) 776-6310

Send an email to Andrea@MakeYourMarkGlobal.com

www.ingramcontent.com/pod-product-compliance
Lightning Source LLC
Chambersburg PA
CBHW071834080526
44589CB00012B/1006